"*Walking Gently on the Earth* is a field honor God with every decision as they traverse an unjust world. With grace and humility Lisa and Megan Anna connect our everyday decisions to the impoverished garment-factory worker in Indonesia, to an unstable climate and to the profiteers of oppression. *Walking Gently* challenges Christianity to become more relevant to an ever hurting world while providing practical steps, thoughtful biblical reflections and hopeful nuggets to inspire along the way. With an increasingly unstable climate and a growing disparity between rich and poor we need this book more than ever."

JASON ALFONSE FILETA, The Micah Challenge USA

"If you're looking for a creation care book by a recent convert to 'religious environmentalism' with some nice stories and a few Bible verses mixed in, this is not the book for you. *Walking Gently on the Earth* has real substance from an academic who walks the walk, who challenges us to respond to the hidden stories behind our lifestyles and choices. Even if you don't agree with everything she writes—and why bother reading a book if you do?—Lisa McMinn will challenge you to think more deeply and more faithfully about life on earth."

RUSTY PRITCHARD, Ph.D., natural resource economist and cofounder of Flourish

"This is a book about change. And hope. Drawing on wisdom from cultures the world over, McMinn and Neff show us that the call to live well as part of God's creation is as urgent as it is ancient, and its faithful pursuit is as much an art as it is a science. By challenging how we see the world, they help us understand, in practical ways, that balance is a thing of beauty, and that celebration and stewardship go hand in hand."

BEN LOWE, activist and author of *Green Revolution*

"This book is a loving and urgent invitation to Christians to fall in love with the earth that God created. Lisa Graham McMinn, assisted by one of her daughters, has deftly woven together an impressive thread of information on how Western culture has divorced us from the land our Creator gave us, and why God calls us back to eating and living in a healthy—physically and spiritually—manner. . . . I heartily recommend this new contribution for those who want to know more and who want to make a difference—walking gently along the way."

MICHAEL MACLEOD, assistant professor of political science,
George Fox University

"In the last five years there have been many books published on the topic concerning a Christian's response to environmental stewardship. . . . This new work, *Walking Gently on the Earth,* now leads the pack. Lisa McMinn is a very gifted communicator with a writing style that is enjoyable and easy to understand. This book is balanced in its presentation of academics blended with common sense—it is challenging and thought-provoking. *Walking Gently on the Earth* is definitely a book for every twenty-first-century Christian to read and contemplate."

TRI ROBINSON, pastor of Vineyard Boise Church
and author of *Small Footprint, Big Handprint*

# WALKING

# GENTLY ON

# THE EARTH

*Making Faithful Choices About*
*Food, Energy, Shelter and More*

LISA GRAHAM MCMINN
AND MEGAN ANNA NEFF

IVP Books
An imprint of InterVarsity Press
Downers Grove, Illinois

InterVarsity Press
P.O. Box 1400, Downers Grove, IL 60515-1426
World Wide Web: www.ivpress.com
E-mail: email@ivpress.com

InterVarsity Press® is the book-publishing division of InterVarsity Christian Fellowship/USA®, a movement of students and faculty active on campus at hundreds of universities, colleges and schools of nursing in the United States of America, and a member movement of the International Fellowship of Evangelical Students. For information about local and regional activities, write Public Relations Dept., InterVarsity Christian Fellowship/USA, 6400 Schroeder Rd., P.O. Box 7895, Madison, WI 53707-7895, or visit the IVCF website at <www.intervarsity.org>.

Unless otherwise indicated, all Scripture quotations are taken from the Holy Bible, New Living Translation, copyright ©1996, 2004. Used by permission of Tyndale House Publishers, Inc., Wheaton, Illinois 60189. All rights reserved.

African artwork by Kirsten McCammon

Cover design: Cindy Kiple
Cover images: Pete Turner/Getty Images

ISBN 978-0-8308-3299-6

Printed in the United States of America ∞

Printed on 100 percent recycled paper.

 green press INITIATIVE   InterVarsity Press is committed to protecting the environment and to the responsible use of natural resources. As a member of Green Press Initiative we use recycled paper whenever possible. To learn more about the Green Press Initiative, visit <www .greenpressinitiative.org>.

**Library of Congress Cataloging-in-Publication Data**

McMinn, Lisa Graham, 1958-
    Walking gently on the earth: making faithful choices about food,
energy, shelter and more / Lisa Graham McMinn and Megan Anna Neff.
        p. cm.
    Includes bibliographical references.
    ISBN 978-0-8308-3299-6 (pbk.: alk. paper)
    1. Human ecology—Religious aspects—Christianity. 2. Christianity
and culture. 3. Creation. 4. Christian stewardship. I. Neff, Megan
Anna, 1984- II. Title.
        BT695.5.M46 2010
        241'.691—dc21

2010014325

| P | 18 | 17 | 16 | 15 | 14 | 13 | 12 | 11 | 10 | 9 | 8 | 7 | 6 | 5 | 4 | 3 | 2 | 1 |
|---|----|----|----|----|----|----|----|----|----|---|---|---|---|---|---|---|---|---|
| Y | 25 | 24 | 23 | 22 | 21 | 20 | 19 | 18 | 17 | 16 | 15 | 14 | 13 | 12 | 11 | 10 |

*For my grandchildren,*
*and yours*
LISA GRAHAM MCMINN

*To Stella Kasiyre, my African mommy,*
*who works tirelessly to bring life, hope and laughter*
*to her neighbors near and far*

*and in memory of Hezekiah Kasiyre,*
*and other children who do not live to their fifth birthdays*
MEGAN ANNA NEFF

# CONTENTS

# PRELUDE

## Siamese Crocodiles

*Funtunfunefu-Denkyemfunefu*

During my second year of seminary I shared a house with two friends. By the second week we had coined names for each of our bedrooms based on the character of the rooms which, incidentally, matched our wardrobes and personalities. We called my room "Ten Thousand Villages" after a non-profit chain that carries fair-trade goods from around the world. My housemates' rooms were "Pottery Barn" and "West Elm." We were an eclectic trio.

My room featured Ghanaian photos hanging on clothespins from my wall, African necklaces, a Malawian wall painting and a Malawian wood table in the corner. Perhaps I make too much show over the fact that I love all things African. The irony is that the classic "Pottery Barn" and "West Elm" rooms—the cream duvet, the black photo frames, the Ikea desk—were just as international as my African room with its paintings and carvings. Whether it is disguised like my housemates' rooms, or obnoxiously over-the-top like mine, most of us live in homes full of

décor from around the world, and have international wardrobes
and food pantries.

I have traveled to many different places in my life, but I will
never come close to visiting all the places my food and clothes
have been. How many places have your taste buds visited today?
Coffee from Indonesia, oranges from Florida, bananas from Honduras, chocolate from Ghana, biscotti from London, tomatoes
from Mexico, rice from Thailand. Our taste buds are tantalized by
food flown from all over the world to our doorstep. And how about
accessories and clothes—how many countries are you wearing today? As I sit here writing, I have a wallet from India beside me, a
coffee mug from China which is filled with a cinnamon dolce soy
latte (I'm sure there are several countries involved in the espresso,
soy, sugar), and I'm wearing a J. Crew dress, also from China.

The fact that our world is becoming increasingly interdependent, that we can flip on the news and hear what is going on in
Sudan, India, France or our local town, shows that we are connected, but not necessarily that we care for one another any more.
Charles W. Forman, a historian and Presbyterian missionary who
taught church history in India, argues in his book *A Faith for the
Nations* that Christ is the only secure basis for human unity. "We
cannot bear the closer contacts and the constant rubbing up against
each other if we do not know clearly how it is that we belong together and whether we are one family. Life together without any
sense of relationship would only be hell for us. It would mean being jammed together with strangers for whom we have no concern
and who have no concern for us. . . . It is this situation that makes
it imperative that we human beings know our unity and know an
immovable foundation on which that unity is established." As the
world grows in its interdependency through economic, political
and cultural systems, it becomes all the more necessary to understand *how* we belong to one another. The question is not whether
or not we are united but what that unity will look like.

Living in Ghana I was often delighted and inspired by the wisdom of Akan culture. For the Akans, symbols have been a rich medium of communication for hundreds of years. They capture essential truths and wisdom, and hold metaphorical meaning; they are most commonly used as designs in decorative cloth and carved into building structures. The meanings of the symbols are derived from a variety of sources: traditional proverbs, historical events, and expressions of particular human attitudes and behaviors.

The *Funtunfunefu-Denkyemfunefu* symbol translated "Siamese Crocodiles" encourages people toward unity marked with love and compassion. It is associated with the proverb *"Funtummireku-denkyemmireku, won afuru bom nso wodidi a na wo pere so,"* translated "two heads fight and struggle though they share one stomach." It would be futile for the crocodiles to fight over their prey, destroying one another over the food that sustains them both. They would be stronger, healthier and generally happier (with far fewer wounds) through a relationship of love and compassion. The crocodiles do not need to strive for unity; it is a fact. We do not need to strive for unity. God has established it by creating an interconnected and interdependent world.

Augustine understood the depth of the kin relationship that God placed upon creation. Forman recounts the story of Augustine chatting with travelers who reported that in the far country they had seen two-headed men. Augustine had no idea whether such men actually existed, but what he did know was that if these men existed they were his brothers in Christ. Augustine grasped that there was no human, no matter how different they might be, who was not his fellow brother or sister in Christ. His firm conviction was that God willed that all should live in unity, loving and caring for each other.

God's will for unity is the secure foundation for it. God doesn't simply suggest unity and love but *wills* them. This foundation goes deeper than human similarities, common interest, cultural knowl-

edge and proximity. It is accepting and acting upon the fact that
we are all brothers and sisters; because of Christ we are *already*
united. We don't need to make it happen; it is already a fact. The
question is not *will* we be unified, but what will the quality of this
unity look like? Will we have relationships modeled after Cain
and Abel, or perhaps Ruth and Naomi?

This compassionate interdependence can be applied to families, friendships, communities, churches or nations. We are united,
whether we like it or not, whether we acknowledge it or not. The
divine act of creation binds us to one another, and the Christian
faith is radical about living lives filled with compassion and love
toward our brothers and sisters. The question is: how do we live
well in a world that is so intimately interconnected and united
that we are like the crocodiles sharing the same core that sustains
us? We are united by political and economic systems, and by our
planet's water, air, oil, copper, coal and soil. To be compassionate
and loving in our unity is to love ourselves *collectively*, to look out
for our own best interests collectively.

Is there any encouragement from belonging to Christ? Any
comfort from his love? Any fellowship together in the Spirit?
Are your hearts tender and compassionate? Then make me
truly happy by agreeing wholeheartedly with each other,
loving one another, and working together with one mind
and purpose.

Don't be selfish; don't try to impress others. Be humble,
thinking of others as better than yourselves. Don't look out
only for your own interests, but take an interest in others, too.

You must have the same attitude that Christ Jesus had.
(Philippians 2:1-5)

# FOR THE BEAUTY
# OF THE EARTH

*It is not possible to love an unseen God*
*while mistreating God's visible creation.*

—JOHN WOOLMAN

The Willamette River's call to come play is nearly irresistible. So on one irresistible summer evening, my daughter Megan Anna and I loaded our kayaks into the pick-up and drove ten minutes to Roger's Landing. In another two minutes we were kayaking downstream. Herons watched us from the shore, and then lifted and glided away when we drew close. A hawk soared overhead, a couple of fish jumped, and more than a few spiders went about the business of catching insects in webs spun under the giant oak tree we floated beneath as we explored a tributary off the river. Old trees soaked gnarled toes at the bank of the river, moss dangling from their fingers, playing with insects on the water's surface. Megan Anna was sure she saw the swirling water trail of an alligator or two, not quite believing my claim that they don't live in the waters of the northwest. We saw evidence of a northwest clan of *homo sapiens:* piers built one hundred years ago for lashing logs together before sending them down to Salem and beyond, springs from a twin bed now so rusted and set in the bank it seemed to be part of the landscape. We left the river with hearts full, renewed in our love of God's good earth—home to so much more than we see on any ordinary day.

On another irresistible summer evening something else altogether came calling. That week our neighbors harvested the conifer trees growing on their property—land they called home and on which they had claim of ownership in a way rather peculiar to *homo sapiens*. It took a rather short time to fell, strip and cart off five acres of forest. We watched the massive felling of two-hundred-foot trees, trunks cracking, branches splintering, ground vibrating as the trees hit earth. With horrid fascination we watched the monstrous machine that picked up trunks like they were twigs, stacking and loading them on trucks that would take them to the mill. In the night displaced insects arrived at our door, swarming around our house in search of a new home. Hundreds of tiny gnats rushed inside when we opened a door to step outside. They died in the night, creating a carpet of black on the wood floors that we vacuumed up the next morning. Yet, our neighbors needed the income, lumberjacks need work, and people like me, watching from the second floor of a home that used a fair amount of lumber in its construction, know my publisher will use trees to publish my book.

Two stories evoking different responses. The first invites reflection to pause, see and celebrate what is awe-inspiring, beautiful, mysterious and consistent in its sameness through the ages. There is sustenance and blessing for our soulish bodies in mountain hikes, starry nights and kayak trips down the Willamette River. The second is an invitation of sorts too. It is an invitation to think deeply about living well in a modern and complex world. We all need earth's resources to survive, but the complexity comes in knowing how brazenly to approach the harvesting of what we need. Descriptions of felling forests, oil spills, strip mining for coal, packing pigs into "feed lots" and stacking laying hens in cages elicit a different set of emotions. Perhaps these provoke defensiveness at a litany that sounds too much like Mother Earth rhetoric, an overvaluing of creation when there are other, more profound human problems confronting us.

Our hope is that whatever emotion this book stirs, it will primarily invite you to celebrate God's good earth and to live in ways that foster the well-being of creation, this beautiful place we call home. Walking gently is a dance of sorts. It includes enjoying the good gifts of this bounteous earth while taking no more than we need. In walking gently we provide for our children—for all children—and for people and creatures yet to be born.

## THE CURRENT CLIMATE

Conversations about caring for God's creation are heating up these days—and not just figuratively. The debate about whether or not global warming is occurring ended in 2007, at least in the political and public sphere in the United States; the debate that remains is whether or not, and how much, humans have caused it. A call to do something about it comes from respected biologists, geologists, ecologists, social scientists, journalists, politicians and community organizers who write articles for *Newsweek, Science, Atlantic Monthly* and *Christianity Today.* Even the airlines are taking note. On a recent trip I took to Chicago, the *AmericanWay* magazine declared itself "the Green Issue" and was chock-full of articles about green building construction, CEOs choosing environmental practices, policies to preserve wetlands and encourage energy alternatives. While flying across the continent, passengers could learn about the value of fluorescent light bulbs, LEED ratings and carbon footprints. There is some irony that an airline industry dependent on a fair amount of fossil fuels is promoting ecological sustainability—but I take hope in whatever form it comes. "Green" shows up as a theme in our movies, in Super Bowl ads, and in grass-roots movements such as Green America that hold rallies and use the Internet to make up-to-date resources available about how to live sustainable lives. Ordinary people are signing petitions and writing letters, working together to change policies in our neighborhoods, grocery stores, churches, corporations and governments.

A lot of those ordinary folks supported the 2009 Disney movie *Earth* by purchasing a ticket. Released on Earth Day, the film became a top-grossing documentary opener, and since the producers agreed to plant a tree for every ticket sold in the first week, 2.7 million trees were to be planted in the fragile rainforest of Brazil. The film follows three animal families for a year as they trek toward hunting or watering grounds to survive. I say "family," but mostly what we see are mamas helping their babies survive. We also see a variety of creatures from the sea, land and air as they nurture, prod, carry, push and encourage babies along the way. We are reminded of other species that call this planet home, and seem to love life, and want to see their babies flourish about as much as we do. A picture *is* worth a thousand words as the film clearly depicts how flourishing is becoming more difficult with global warming. Polar bear families in the Arctic are losing the sheets of ice they need as platforms for summer hunting, elephant families are losing water needed to survive in the deserts of Africa, strange and beautiful birds are losing their habitat in the earth's rain forests.

So yes, okay, we're supposed to appreciate creation. After all, God created earth and its creatures, called it "very good," and seemingly entrusted it into the care of humans. But a lot of us aren't sure what *caring* for it means besides appreciating stars and sunsets and recycling our newspapers. Even if we're convinced we need to do something differently than we've been doing the last hundred years, we feel mostly stuck. We need our cars to drive to work, and don't necessarily have the time, know-how or energy to grow a vegetable garden.

Feeling stuck comes naturally enough. It took a couple of generations to trade in our knowledge about how to live off the land for comfort and convenience. It happened so gradually we didn't much notice. Besides, we didn't have to be overly concerned about industries that dumped sewage into rivers since, for most of history, the human population stayed relatively small and our impact didn't amount to much. Our great-grandparents or even grandparents didn't drive an average of forty miles a day, eat imported tomatoes in January, and ship tons (a lot of tons) of corn and lumber around the globe. The world population and industrial expansion pretty much grew up together, and now we're like giant adolescents tromping around the vegetable patch and mucking up the water supply, *although none of us want to be doing so.*

As Christians living in the West, some of us have tended to believe that earth is a temporary home that will one day pass away. Since saving souls has mattered more than saving matter (whether human, whale or tree), we've justified using this way station called earth however we've seen fit so long as we're working on saving souls. Earth has been seen as God's gift to sustain us until we reach our final destination, where a new heaven and earth await. This separation of the spiritual from the physical has meant that we've sometimes pitted caring for creation against caring for people.

Caring for people has been a high priority for the church. *But in the twenty-first century we can't adequately care for people without giving some good attention to caring for earth.* For most of human history earth has provided a seemingly endless supply of resources, but in the last twenty-five years articles in reputable, peer-reviewed scientific journals have been showing us that we no longer inhabit a planet with unlimited resources and an endless capacity to absorb the byproducts of our lives. Caring for people, it appears, must now include caring about climate change, deforestation and species extinctions.

African professor and theologian J. O. Y. Mante says attending to creation is the foundation of all disciplines that are serious about life. Mante says Western theology is ecologically bankrupt. We spend our best theological energy talking about abstract doctrines such as sanctification, or covenants and dispensations, and leave little energy for talking about doctrines connected to living life. The result is that we live a non-ecological existence that is gradually destroying both human and nonhuman life. How, Mante asks, is that Christian? African theology begins by talking about the fundamentals of life that infuse how Christians live—a theology of food, a theology of power. If we are willing to be humble we may learn something of our blind spots by attending to insights that come from Christians outside our own culture.

Thankfully, Westerners *are* already engaging in this conversation. Lester Brown, president of Earth Policy Institute, has developed a comprehensive plan for turning us around, a global plan that requires global action. Continuing as we have takes us nowhere good—and fairly rapidly in the big span of time. The bad news, according to Brown, is that we are destroying the world that supports our economy and well-being. The good news is that our political systems have potential power to bring about significant change and are beginning to lean into that change.

While Brown calls us to global action, he knows that change starts with compelling people to look out for their own and their children's well-being. Christians following Jesus' command to love our neighbor as ourselves can become leaders in this effort to look beyond our own well-being to that of our local and global neighbors. What if Christians became models for loving our neighbors by choosing to live more sustainable lives that don't use more than our share of earth's resources? What a witness to the world we could be, glorifying God and pointing people to Jesus.

It is easy for me to feel shame or guilt about how I live, but those don't motivate me to change nearly so much as when I feel *inspired* to change. Maybe you feel the same. The writer of Hebrews tells us to encourage each other to perseverance and hope. Let's hold tightly to the hope we say we have, while bursting with love and good deeds (see Hebrews 10:23-24). Love can compel us to grow both our passion for the abundant life that God desires for all and a virtue of care that considers the food we eat, as well as the energy and stuff we consume.

## GROWING PASSION FOR THE WHOLE EARTH

A group of boys at Lowell Elementary School, the school I attended during my childhood years in Arizona, spent recess raiding black ants from a black ant pile and dumping them onto a red ant pile. I once watched the battle play out. The outnumbered black ants were mercilessly attacked, bitten and pulled in half, slaughtered, to the glee of the boys. The memory of it pains me still—forty-some years later. The motives of boys who randomly killed horned toads, turtles and snakes didn't make sense to me. I figured God intended desert creatures to enjoy their lives too.

Perhaps senseless killing pained me so much because my father encouraged me to notice and love God's creation. I grew up admiring sunsets, poking around in caves and imagining life on other planets while looking at the stars from our roof. We nursed a few wounded birds and squirrels back to health along the way, and tried to discourage Dragon Lady, our family dog, from killing things right alongside the neighborhood boys.

But despite my distaste for the tormenting of any creature, I always figured a person could still be a devout Christian even if they enjoyed staging wars between ant colonies. Caring for earth was a matter of personal choice, I thought, a passion some folks had, but not essential to faith.

While God's grace is certainly large enough to cover children and adults who take life and creation lightly, I don't see caring for creation as optional anymore. Noticing and loving creation reflects respect for and receptivity to God. Earth is a place of beauty, blessing, diversity and delight, where all the pieces fit together into a complete whole. Calling earth *good* acknowledges and embraces our interdependence with other creatures and our kinship with nonhuman neighbors that share our forests, oceans, prairies and jungles. Theologian Steven Bouma-Prediger says:

> God's creatures are valuable not because of their usefulness to humans—though some are useful, indeed essential, to us. Instead they are valuable to each other—for example, the cedars are valuable as places for birds to nest, and the mountains are valuable as places of refuge and rest for wild goats—and most important rocks and trees, birds and animals are valuable simply because God made them. Value rests in being creations of a valuing God—not in their being a means to some human end.

This conversation cuts across generations. Increasingly the students in my classes at the Christian university where I teach are saying they believe we should be responsible stewards of creation, so long as we keep Mother Earth off a pedestal. Christians young and old are becoming convinced that living with an ecological worldview is *implicitly* Christian.

A small class met at my house on alternate Monday nights one spring to discuss books and big ideas. One night our conversation turned to food. "Let's suppose that eating has something to do with our faith," I said. Since five of the nine students had little knowledge about—and generally little interest in—cooking, and two had grown up in cook-free homes where they primarily ate fast food, take-out and packaged or processed meals, the students didn't know what to do with a conversation that suggested what they ate might have something to do with ecology, and perhaps even their faith.

Given that possibility, and the likelihood that the stuff they buy, the fuel they consume and their family size choices are somehow expressions of their faith, students are increasingly leaning into these conversations. As the professor, I've asked myself what students need to know to engage these cultural questions well, in a way that is informed by their faith. That question drives the approach of this book.

Three kinds of information help us engage these questions well. First, we need to know some of the backstory about issues being debated in our local papers, on the national news and at international summits. Along with some of the history of a particular conversation, we need to understand the cultural values that incline a group of people (including ourselves!) to react one way or another to an issue.

Second, we need to know how to check for inconsistencies in how our faith bumps up against our culture's values—which is a Very Difficult task indeed. Trying to do this by yourself is like trying to remove a leech from your back. A stick might help, as might rubbing your back against a tree or the ground, but the best way to get a leech off your back is to get someone else to remove it for you. The "someone else" could be Christians in other parts of the world, people who share our faith but not necessarily our history, and subsequent worldview and cultural values. As you've already seen in Megan Anna's first prelude, we'll be introducing you to some African Christian worldviews and cultural values along the way.

Third, we need to know what we can do about it. Information without tangible, practical suggestions can become disheartening and downright *un*helpful. We will have failed if you end this book wanting to be a better citizen of earth yet feeling helpless and hopeless about where to start. So we include a lot of practical tools about how to begin, or how to take the next step, or the next one after that if you are walking gently already.

The most challenging of these three tasks is the second—seeing where our Christian worldview has been shaped more by cultural values and context than our faith. Understanding the backstory or having a pocket full of practical tools won't motivate us nearly as much as being convinced that living differently will bring congruency to our faith and lifestyle choices.

Everyone's thoughts about how they are connected to earth are embedded in their particular culture's ideas of what it means to live well and responsibly. For example, I'm guessing that a number of you would need a fair bit of convincing to believe that being good stewards of God's creation is as foundational to being Christian as, say, evangelism. What if the belief that evangelism is more important than creation care is influenced by our Western culture instead of being a core Christian belief that transcends time and place? Here's my opening shot at supporting why being good stewards is as foundational to being Christian as, for example, evangelism.

## THREE REASONS WHY WALKING GENTLY IS ABOUT BEING CHRISTIAN

In response to the question "What is the greatest commandment?" Jesus answered, "'You must love the LORD your God with all your heart, all your soul, all your mind, and all your strength.' The second is equally important: 'Love your neighbor as yourself.' No other commandment is greater than these" (Mark 12:30-31). I heard Sandress Misska, a Malawian theologian and the country director of World Relief, speak on this passage. His explanation of this verse is the first reason caring for earth is foundational to being a Christian: *To love God with our heart, soul and mind is to love others as ourselves. One way of showing love to others is by caring for their physical well-being.*

Christians have a strong legacy of caring for people; we take seriously the command to love our neighbor as ourselves. Around the world Christians have built orphanages, hospitals and schools. And Christians support organizations like World Vision, World

Relief, Habitat for Humanity and The Heifer Project, redistributing wealth by bringing food, shelter, clothing and livelihoods to the people living on little around the world. Biblical teachings, such as the good Samaritan story, encourage us to care for others by caring for their physical well-being. In the Gospel of Matthew Jesus describes God gathering the nations and judging them according to how they treated the hungry, the naked, the sick and the stranger (Matthew 25:31-46), and the New Testament writer James said our faith was dead if we didn't prove it by our actions (James 2:15-17).

But the Western church split over what loving others looked like in the early twentieth century. Christians who focused on love through meeting physical needs went one direction (social gospel folks) and Christians who focused on love through evangelism went the other (evangelical and fundamentalist folks). Being "progressive" or "conservative" said as much about our politics as our understanding of what it meant to be Christian—and politics and faith became entangled in unhelpful ways. Saving bodies and souls should never have been separated, and a mending of sorts is occurring now, nearly one hundred years later, but the tension and suspicion linger for evangelicals and fundamentalists. This tension means some hold creation care at arm's length, not wanting to lose sight of the importance of evangelism in caring overly much for physical needs.

Let's assume we are to care for the body and soul as an inseparable whole. In that case, to care for bodies as well as souls in the twenty-first century will likely require a reevaluation of how we live. At our point in history loving others depends on our attending to creation because people's well-being depends on a healthy planet. Loving others may require us to take and use no more than we need, and to do so in ways that do not harm what others need to flourish.

A second reason caring for earth is foundational to what it

means to be Christian is because *we are creatures of earth, and so caring for earth is a way of caring for ourselves*. We eat what grows from dirt to live. We drink what flows from rivers. I grew up understanding God gave earth to humans to pretty much develop the place and run it. We weren't *part* of earth; we owned it! Because we were made in God's image, we sat above and apart from the rest of creation. We were supposed to fill it with humans who would ideally love God and each other and creatively manipulate earth and animals to meet our needs. Nate Jones, who has spent more than half of his life in Indonesia, is persuaded by another interpretation of Genesis 1:28. He sees it as a great commission of the Old Testament:

> Instead of exercising our dominion to kill off our ecological competitors and replace them with a teeming humanity, we are to fulfill the earth, bringing forth its latent potential and perhaps weaving wild lives and landscapes into a productive and peaceable whole. Certainly, the commission instructs us to lead the creatures of the earth into fulfillment with one another, with ourselves, and with our common Creator. Our first calling, then, is to garden the earth.

Maybe we don't own earth at all. Folk wisdom suggests that people who claim to own land are like fleas who claim to own the dog on which they happen to be hitching a ride and snacking on in the meantime. Sure, the flea might *think* it owns the dog, and a bunch of fleas could wreak havoc on a dog, but those outside the flea population (other dogs, or perhaps humans) would think a flea claiming to own a dog a ridiculous notion. For one thing, the dog is going to outlast the flea, and if it doesn't (if it, let's say, gets hit by a car), the flea's cushy life will be severely compromised anyway. Since the flea depends on the dog for sustenance, it seems a bit audacious for it to claim to be the dog's master and owner.

We are physically part of earth and dependent on it. We don't choose to exist in a dynamic relationship with creation; it is simply a fact of our existence, though one that is surprisingly easy to forget. We have a unique place in creation as image-bearers of God, but we are *of* the soil, of earth nevertheless. Maybe we should see ourselves as gardeners, rather than conquerors. Maybe "filling the earth" was more a commission to nurture and cultivate earth's potential to be a garden full of life rather than a mandate to populate it with humans who would be in charge.

A third reason creation care is foundational to being Christian is that care for earth is an expression of respect and receptivity to God because *God made it, loves it and called it good—good enough, in fact, that God became flesh and dwelled among us* (John 1:14). For God so loved the world, *cosmos*, the entire universe, that he gave his only son, Jesus (John 3:16), that the world might be restored, redeemed, made right. We honor and worship God when we live in ways that reflect God's love for, and sustaining role as caretaker of, creation. How could we not love what God loves? Earth is our home. God made it for all earth's creatures. A new heaven and a new earth await, and while we don't know quite what that will look like, Quaker philosopher and poet Arthur Roberts pictures a new earth that is familiar—perhaps with places like Niagara Falls, Mount Kilimanjaro, the Nile River and the Amazon—but fully, completely, beautifully restored.

This conversation elicits strong reactions. Sometimes I follow letters to the editor in magazines that have tackled highly volatile subjects about climate change and limiting carbon emissions, population control and the humane treatment of animals. In both religious and nonreligious magazines some of the most inflammatory letters have been written by people identifying themselves as Christian. The inflammatory letter writers find these conversations offensive and misguided—deviating from a biblical call for humans to subdue and dominate creation, and to be fruitful and multiply, filling the earth. Perhaps some of the response reflects fear that our culture is turning toward earth worship. Perhaps it also reflects ways that Western values of manifest destiny, growth, power and independence have come to define what it means to be Christian.

## WHERE WE ARE GOING

I want to believe that the inflammatory letter writers are in the minority. The more I talk with people, the more I realize they care about ecological questions but feel overwhelmed by what they don't know, and by the hugeness of the problems. *Walking Gently* is a primer that helps Christians understand some basic issues, offers ideas about how to live gently and inspires hope. We argue for an ecological worldview that celebrates this earth as God's good gift, and then invites you to celebrate the goodness of earth by living with an ethic of care. Since some of our best models for walking gently come from the Global South, we infuse our ideas with their wisdom. Megan Anna has spent time in Malawi and Ghana, becoming a student of their worldviews, and at Princeton Seminary she immersed herself in the study of African Christian theology. She opens each chapter with a prelude introducing some nugget of wisdom from the Global South blended with theological reflection. Lisa writes the chapters, some of which offer more of the backstory, some of which offer more practical steps; most of them include both, as well as ways to examine your thinking as it is informed by your faith. Most chapters conclude with a resource section to help guide you toward next steps, and a couple of appendices give those of you who want it more to chew on. You'll notice that most of the resources can be accessed through the Internet. We all have information at our fingertips, though sifting through reliable sources can be challenging!

o    o    o

I take a morning walk up Williamson Road where I can see Mt. Hood's majestic silhouette before the sun crests the horizon. My trek takes me past forests, orchards and pastures. Farmland and vineyards pepper the hillsides across the valley. Sometimes I try to imagine how God sees and loves the hawks, deer, coyotes, oak, fir, cows, sheep, horses and people represented in this space. It isn't easy—most of the details are invisible to me. But maybe if we could all see the world a little more like God does we would walk in it more gently.

Maybe God sees earth bubbling with life just beneath the surface as spring sun warms the soil, and readies bulbs, roots and seeds for bursting forth in new growth. God would see the worms working their way through soil, breaking up clods, leaving residue from their wormy digestion that fosters dark, rich soil. God might also see a robin, a first-year mother flying low, eager to provide food for her newly hatched babies. If God sees it all, God might pay particular attention to a useful, happy worm that comes up to greet the sun (it is spring after all, the season when worms go wild with happiness). The robin sees it too, and engages in a fight for life, pulling tenaciously at the worm until successfully yanking it from the soil, giving it one magnificent moment to experience earth from above before alighting on her nest and feeding it to three young robins with beaks wide open in anticipation.

Oh to see and love the world as God does, in all of its complexity, beauty, sparkling clarity and color! Is God more sad, we might ask, for the worm that died, or happy for the mother and her babies who just filled their tummies? Perhaps that is the wrong question—the question that leads us to put ourselves justifiably at the top of the food chain, and the top of God's list of creation favorites. Perhaps God would have us ask what kind of world is required to see that flourishing continue—for worms (who do amazing things to enrich our soil), for birds who spread seeds, for coyotes, sheep, cows, oak trees, whales. Yes, perhaps even for whales. God sees it all, loves it all and wills for the flourishing of humans—and the flourishing of all.

# PRELUDE

## Strength Lies in Unity

*Nkonsonkonson*

Sitting in a dark restaurant in Thailand I ate chicken. My careful bites around the intact claw reminded me that I was indeed eating a chicken—probably one that was happily eating bugs in the yard just a few hours before. This connection between the animal's life and the meat that I now consumed made me thankful for the chicken that died in order that I might enjoy my lunch in this floral-patterned, dusky restaurant in the rural town of Ubon.

Fast-forward a few years to the Princeton Seminary dining hall and the nondescript pieces of meat on my friends' plates. I asked my friend, "Is that pork or beef?" We had no idea. We lacked any connection to the meat being eaten and the animal that had lived. I searched for a word to describe this lack of regard, or awareness, we had. *Dehumanized* doesn't quite work because animals aren't humans. (Isn't it interesting that we don't even have a word for dehumanizing animals?) By forgetting that the meat represented a life, perhaps we had *de-beinged* this cow or pig that had given itself for us; it was just there—mine for consuming with no need to consider any of the true costs of making it available to me. If I have the money to buy this entrée, don't I deserve to eat it without thinking overly much about where it came from? Isn't that even part of what I'm paying for—the luxury of being removed from the work and sacrifice that went into the meal?

Countries in the Southern Hemisphere (Africa, South America, Southeast Asia) often share more connection between animals and the meat they eat because the link between the life of the animal and the food that is consumed has few gaps. A sacredness and honor is given to life. The traditional religion of the Akans in Ghana acknowledges the living *beings* of cows, chickens, pigs and fish, appreciating all living beings, from the trees to humans. This worldview reverences all life and rarely neglects to appreciate the animals that form and supplement their diet.

Listening to the voices of African Christianity, I grow in my appreciation for life and awareness of all of life. I begin to see how all of creation is connected. The birds and wind that spread seed; the soil that gives the seed a fertile place to germinate; the sun, air and rain that help the seed turn into something that bears fruit for animals and people. Bees pollinate. Spiders live off insects that would otherwise prematurely kill tender plants. We are all interconnected and belong to the whole that is God's creation.

The *nkonsonkonson* symbol is a picture of a chain link representing the strength that lies in unity. The strength of a chain depends on the individual units linked together. While traditionally this symbol refers to human relationships and the importance of contributing to one's community, it can also be applied to the systems of earth that sustain us. I am not above it all, a human director of plant and animal life. Rather, I am an integral part of this grand symphony of creation, which only God transcends.

Since the industrial revolution, with its developments in technology and changing business practices, people in the Western world have begun to think of humans as being *over* creation rather than an integral *part* of creation. This way of thinking eased its way into the Western mind through the work of Enlightenment philosophers, such as René Descartes. Due to our reason and ability for rational thought, Descartes elevated humans above all other creatures as the only *real being*, while the rest of the world became "things." Enlightenment philosophers have had a lasting impact on our thinking—for good and for ill. Try this little experiment. Open a file in Microsoft Word and type the following sentence: A mother who cares for her children is a great blessing. Now try this: A bear who cares for her cubs is a great blessing. You'll notice that a green squiggly line shows up in the second sentence under the word *who*. According to our English language, an animal is a *that;* only a person gets to be a *who*.

A danger of turning living beings into things is that the "things" easily become consumable objects subject to an all-encompassing economic paradigm. If something is considered economically useless it is discarded (for instance, a male chick hatched at a laying hen hatchery is quickly "discarded" after leaving the shell and being identified as a male). It also means that being "fiscally responsible" is squeezing every bit of economic advantage from each *thing* in order to maximize profits. This economic paradigm changes the way we look at animals. It's easy to be more concerned with the cost of a carton of eggs than with where the eggs come from. Did they come from a hen that (or who) lived her life in a cage entangled with other hens?

The traditional African view of the world understands humanity as part of nature and in an interdependent relationship with nature. Nature is made up of living *beings*, rather then inanimate *things* that are to be used in an endless pursuit. In Africans' view, since the well-being of people is dependent on the well-being of all of creation, the relationship between humanity and nature is harmonious—one of *relationship* rather than one of exploitation. Until the last couple hundred years, Christianity had largely developed and grown from within this more traditional view. With the Enlightenment and the industrial revolution, Christianity in the West came to be more shaped by economic values based on efficiency and growth. As Christianity grows in the Global South, we in the West are being encouraged to rediscover Christianity from the traditional worldview. The Global South is reminding the Western world of our roots, and of hope in a gospel of redemption for the whole cosmos.

# FARMING
# PRACTICES

*Athey was not exactly, or not only, what is called a "landowner."*

*He was the farm's farmer, but also its creature and belonging.*

*He lived its life, and it lived his; he knew that, of the two lives,*

*his was meant to be the smaller and the shorter.*

—WENDELL BERRY, *JAYBER CROW*

My mother and her siblings grew up raising sugar beets in Fort Morgan, Colorado—on one of the six million family farms that provided food for the rest of the nation. Grandma sold eggs from their chickens and cream from the dairy cow to buy fabric to make school dresses for Mom and her sisters. Grandma also tended the large vegetable garden that fed her family along with the chickens and cows they raised.

According to the U.S. Department of Agriculture, in 1930 about one out of every four people in the United States lived on a farm. Now less than two out of every one hundred live on farms, and three-fourths of our food comes from about 157,000 large farms.

We've grown from communities that bought each other's eggs, tomatoes and beef to communities that import beef raised in Brazil and tomatoes grown in Mexico and buy eggs laid in factory farms in Iowa. Our ideas about food and values shifted, accommodating to changes in how we went about the business of growing and raising our food. This chapter explores the backstory and implications of those cultural shifts, especially around the push for and support of all kinds of growth, as well as some things we can do today to slow it down. The next chapter offers practical ways to make our food choices compassionate ones in our current food culture.

## THE AGRICULTURAL GROWTH SPURT

As we transitioned away from family farms to agribusiness we grew in just about every way feasible. Oil discovered during and just following World War II motivated innovation and industry. After the war, science labs built to develop weapons found another focus—creating uses for petroleum. Petroleum-based fertilizers, pesticides and herbicides grew the farming industry, and carpets and hoses, hair dryers and cosmetics, cleaning supplies and paints, toys and hot tubs, recycling containers and trash bags, and the credit cards we used to purchase it all expanded markets, exploding out of innovation and the abundance of petroleum. Cars and trucks became a significant consumer of surplus oil. President Eisenhower signed the Federal Aid Highway Act in 1956, and now our roads are all grown up. We have an Interstate Highway System that allows us to get up and move whenever we get a hankering to do so, and permits trucks to haul oranges from Florida to Maine and strawberries from California to New York.

Our farms grew up too, with the average size (in acres) more than doubling between 1950 and 2000. Farmers in the 1960s and 1970s had to get big or get out. Small family farms went the way of the horse and buggy, and large-scale agribusiness came of age. While family farms like my mother's grew and raised a variety of foods (now referred to as *polyculture*), with consolidation farming transitioned into monoculture industries, and pastures, pens and barnyards were plowed under to make room for one specialized crop. The cows, pigs and chickens went to factory farms that specialized in raising only one kind of animal, saving both time and money over raising them on family farms.

Corn became a crop of choice. Food companies found new ways to feed us the extra corn—corn chips, corn cereals and, most notably, high fructose corn syrup, which replaced sugar as a less expensive sweetener for manufactured drinks and foods. Most vending machines could be called "corn vending machines," though usually the corn is repackaged in a way that disguises it.

Growth in agribusiness distanced us from the raising, harvesting and preparing of our own food. By the turn of the twenty-first century, food growing and tending processes had become largely invisible to most of us, and a cultural value associated with participating in one's food gathering, canning, drying and preparing had shifted toward a cultural value of efficiency.

The shift from small family farms to large agribusiness changed how food was grown as well as what we ate, how we prepared food and how we thought about it. We were snookered by the food industry that convinced women that to be liberated they needed to be free from the dreary task of cooking. We agreed with the makers of such products as Duncan Hines cake mixes and Chef Boyardee spaghetti that making our own food "from scratch" wasted creative energy that could be better spent making money. Buying boxed mixes and canned dinners became a measure of our economic success, placing us securely in America's middle class. Almost without noticing we came to depend on the convenience of Captain Crunch, Swanson dinners and SpaghettiOs.

## CONNECTING TO THE HARVEST

I buy a bag of brown rice and don't know anything about where it is grown, much less the women, men and children involved in

growing and harvesting it. The same was true when I bought
boneless, skinless chicken breasts packaged in yellow Styrofoam
trays wrapped in cellophane. Not having to work around claws
and feathers, gizzards and beaks used to seem like a definite
plus—and, at the time, so did the fact that my children had no
idea that our dinner once bore any resemblance to Chicken Little.
I'm fairly sure our daughters thought *chicken*, as in the animal that
clucks, was an entirely different thing than *chicken*, as in McNug-
gets. I'm not proud of this.

That any of us still purchase Thanksgiving turkeys that actually look something like the bird we're eating surprises me a bit,
though I do recall hearing a few "eeew" and "yuck" expletives
along the holiday dinner prep path as my daughters helped me
dress the turkey. For our family, disgust has turned to awareness
of animals—their lives and sacrifice that we might eat meat. The
last time we cooked a turkey for Thanksgiving, Megan Anna reminded us that Native Americans approached an animal they had
hunted and shot, and thanked it, recognizing the animal died so
that they might be nourished. So in our thanksgiving prayer we
thanked God for the turkey, acknowledging the sacrifice of the
turkey for our Thanksgiving feast.

Since I've never had to grow my own food, I don't tend to be
particularly mindful of farm workers' labor that brings the sweet
potatoes, peas, cranberries and olives to the store so I can serve
them at my Thanksgiving table. A Thanksgiving experience had
greater significance when families gathered with thankfulness for
the bounty they had worked for, celebrating the end of the harvesting, canning, drying and storing of meats, vegetables, grains
and fruits that would carry their families through the winter
months. The labors of people and the sacrifice of animals became
inconsequential as we became increasingly removed from agricultural processes.

The summer my parents moved us all back to our roots in Oregon I experienced firsthand the hard work and fun of farm life. Oregon's youth harvested summer crops before child labor laws prohibited it, and schools finished up in early June so farmers could count on pickers when the strawberries ripened. My siblings and I picked strawberries for Mr. and Mrs. Love, packing our lunch the night before and then rising early to catch an old school bus pulled out of retirement for the weeks of summer harvest. We'd bend over our rows, picking berries as we moved down the mounds of green laden with red, fragrant berries, sometimes visiting with whoever was picking the next row over (or, in the case of the rebellious few, chucking rotten strawberries at whoever was in range when no one was looking). More often each of us stayed captivated by our own thoughts and the stories we made up in our heads as we filled our flats. We could eat what we wanted but only got paid for what we turned in, and so after the first day or two, eating fresh strawberries took a distant second place to productivity.

I learned something about food during those summer weeks. But over the years I forgot things I knew and appreciated back then—especially the labor-intensive process of harvesting fragile berries, and how the perfectly ripe strawberry bursts in your mouth with a flavor reserved for warm berries right off the bush.

My siblings and I also helped harvest hazelnuts and walnuts on the orchard of my eventual in-laws during Octobers through high school. They hired the church youth group kids to come rake the hazelnut crop into piles and pick up the walnuts that had fallen, ready for harvesting. We were given Snickers or Mars candy bars for a morning snack, Coke or Dr Pepper in the afternoon, and we'd break for lunch and sit around chatting and flirting until we headed back to the orchard. I treasure my few forays into the communal ritual of harvesting.

Mark and I could have done more to expose our children to harvesting. We could have driven to U-Pick farms and picked apples, peaches or berries. These days Mark and I go down the road a couple of miles to the Smiths to pick our blueberries. We take just an hour on two July summer mornings to get what we'll freeze and use for the year. The Smiths use an honor system for payment, so we weigh our berries on the scale when we're done and drop our money in the metal box attached to the shed. We pay about half of what we would if we bought blueberries at Ray's Produce Stand, and one could argue that our time is worth more than that. But for us, connecting to harvesting is not about saving money but about staying mindful of the laborers that provide us with most of our food, and of God's scheme to bless earth's inhabitants with new food every year from dirt, sun, water, plants and maybe a bee or two. Besides, Mark and I find it peaceful to spend an hour picking berries in the cool of a summer morning. We think simple thoughts as we listen to the birds, and only partly hear the cars zipping by on Highway 240.

## THE PLUS SIDE OF EFFICIENCY

Lest you think otherwise, I do acknowledge advantages that came with the efficiency of agribusiness. Food got less expensive, and we could produce a lot of it to feed our growing population.

The free enterprise system works because competition for your dollars and mine keeps business owners motivated to improve their products and to produce them more efficiently—for less cost. The competition for food dollars led to a race to lower costs of producing food and, subsequently, the price of food for us. The Brown farm can sell their eggs for less than the Green farm and still stay in business if they can find ways to cut the costs of producing eggs. Efficiency won the day.

Most farmers in Yamhill and Washington counties now use machines to rake and gather hazelnuts and walnuts. It's noisy, and fills the orchard with the smell of gasoline and machinery—but it's efficient. Keeping laying hens in cages off the ground, rather than in barnyards, meant one could manage a lot of hens. Feeding, poop clean-up and egg collection is managed easily with conveyer belts and set feeding and watering systems, eliminating three time-consuming jobs and allowing egg producers to sell a lot of eggs at low cost. Bringing cows (and pigs) into feedlots and fattening them up fast with corn is far more efficient than being limited by the number of cows one could feed by pasturing and waiting four years for them to put on enough weight to take them to market. Once the industrial engines took hold of the food production business, ample food could be grown, processed and distributed with less human labor, and at less cost to you and me.

The story typically gets told positively—and what's not to like about it? Fewer people had to perform tedious toil simply to survive. People were freed to expand their creative potential because they could pursue other occupational interests. Instead of everyone being a jack-of-all trades like my grandparents—who grew sugar beets, milked cows, made their own butter, shoed their horse, gathered eggs, canned fruit, slaughtered their chickens, and made their own egg noodles and clothes—people could specialize. Some managed or worked in canneries, others owned or worked in slaughterhouses and meat packaging plants, but most turned to nonrelated food jobs. Some worked as seamstresses in the garment industry, or in the ever-expanding assembly lines where all kinds of products were being developed and made for mass distribution. Eventually most of those jobs went overseas, so more of us now work in service industries. We are teachers, therapists, nurses, sales representatives, hair stylists, personal trainers, consultants, marketers, financial advisers, social workers and civil servants. The human ingenuity that ushered us into the industrial revolution with the steam engine carried us into the information age with computer and wireless technology.

Our food comes to us efficiently. We have many choices and much convenience, and spend less on food than our grandparents and great-grandparents did before and just after World War II.

More of our monthly budget can go for drinking mochas with friends, updating our wardrobe or wireless technology, and maybe even springing for tickets to a concert or basketball game. This is not a bad thing. But progress and growth did bring some consequences that were *not* so good.

## THE HIDDEN COSTS OF LOW-COST FOOD

The efficiency and growth of the food industry also meant that in every decade from 1920 through the end of the century the number of family farms in the United States declined. This was especially noticeable by 1970, when the growth and efficiency of large farms out-competed families who were trying to make a living off small farms and who saw the price of their crops sink beneath what it cost to grow them.

Large-scale agribusiness expanded into farming communities by buying up small-scale family farms and creating consolidated businesses. Most farmers sold their farms and migrated to cities, joining the expanding urban and suburban American population. Farms that made it into the twenty-first century largely valued growth, progress, efficiency and technological innovation, and the most viable farms today are part of large businesses that employ managers, supervisors and farm laborers. Because so much low-cost food is produced, agribusinesses can transport it across the continent, or oceans, at what seem to be reasonable prices to people pushing carts up and down the aisles of Piggly Wiggly or Safeway. We've become used to having pineapples, oranges and fresh beef year round, to shopping for specials on milk and canned corn, and to getting Thanksgiving turkeys for thirty-nine cents a pound. We value lots of choices and competitive bargains, and have come to expect them from our grocers.

As the distance grew between the steer raised on the farm and the ground beef wrapped in cellophane and stacked with other meat products in the grocery store, we didn't feel like we had lost anything worth keeping. Besides, the lower prices made us happy meat consumers. We bought the goods that came with progress and felt proud of our country's good fortune.

But some hidden costs of low-cost food have been exposed, raising questions that won't go away. Maybe the questions are troubling because they bump up against what it means to be God's compassionate and merciful representatives on earth.

*Animal misery.* Mark didn't used to believe a chicken could be "unhappy." He didn't think chickens had the brainpower necessary to compute either happiness or misery. Maybe they don't in the way that humans do, but Mark now knows a happy hen when he sees one, as well as one he would describe as living in misery. We acquired our first brood of chicks during the writing of this book, and shortly after that, while driving through our hometown of Newberg we came alongside a truck carrying hens packed into cages. Patches of bare skin showed through where feathers had been worn away, one visible sign to car passengers of a stressed life in a crowded wire cage absent of bedding, dirt or perches. Chickens usually have beady lively eyes; these lacked any spark of life. They fell into each other as the truck stopped and started, looking apathetic, dull, unresponsive. We were witnessing misery or, at the very least, the absence of life beyond the most biological definition. The image haunts us still.

One uncomfortable question arising from unintended consequences of growth in the food industry is the treatment of animals. For a long time I turned away from stories about Concentrated Animal Feeding Operations (CAFOs). I liked animals well enough, but believed God gave them to us to use responsibly and well—which included eating some of them. Animal rights folks were raving radicals, I thought, and I'd change the channel or turn the page or round the corner to avoid them. It took me a while to be willing to sit with and sift through information honestly. I hoped to conclude the tales were mostly an exaggeration since the tendency to multiply woes abounds in all controversial areas. And some exaggeration is here as well. But after reading a variety of perspectives I could not deny that CAFOs and egg-producing factory farms are unhappy places for animals.

For instance, we call hens in the egg industry "laying hens," and hens and roosters in the meat industry "broilers," and in doing so render all their other creaturely activities irrelevant. Yet God gave a hen a natural desire to care for her young. She builds a nest in preparation of them, and is a patient "nester." She rotates her eggs up to five times a day as they gestate, and then watches over her hatched chicks, feeding them and gathering them under her wings for protection and warmth. In her spare time she dust-bathes, perches and forages, exploring the world through her beak. This nurturing animal is the most mistreated in factory farming.

Between half and two-thirds of her beak will be cut off, causing physical pain as bone, cartilage, soft tissue and nerve endings are cut through. Clipping, or debeaking, is done to keep her from pecking her neighbors out of the crazed madness that comes from being bored and crowded with a bunch of unhappy hens. She can't spread her wings; she can hardly turn around in a circle, and of course there is no nesting, dust-bathing or foraging. The space allotted to her to live out her life as a laying hen is smaller than a piece of paper. She never hatches and cares for her young, but the instinct to reproduce is so strong that it drives her to keep laying eggs, which is, after all, to our benefit. She experiences misery her whole life. Which at least is rather short compared to hens in barnyards. Near the end of it (about a year), when her production drops off, her caretakers (I use this word very loosely) stop feeding and watering her, which stimulates her body to put forth one final wave of egg-laying before she is removed from the production line and sent to slaughter for stews and pot pies.

I won't go into such detail again, but neither will I apologize for it here. The value in removing the veil of ignorance that protects consumers from animal misery is making the invisible visible. When we see what is, we can make more intentional choices about what we will or will not support.

I became willing to look at the reality of how animals in the food industry are treated after our daughter Sarah became a vegan. She invited Mark and me to understand why—not pushing information on us, but making resources available to us when we asked for them. After doing some reading and thinking, we challenged cultural values we had adopted that made it acceptable to treat animals as simple commodities. Now I assume greater responsibility to figure out what it means to respect and care well for animals, particularly those from whom I plan to take something— whether honey, eggs or a life. One thing is sure: meat, eggs and dairy will cost more, because efficiency is traded in for respectful care of animals, which requires more time and more space.

**Unsound agricultural practices.** That CAFOs are environmentally unsound and unsustainable is another hidden cost of growth. For instance, that single pound of beef I brown before adding it to spaghetti took about 2,500 gallons of water to produce. Moreover, the groundwater pollution that comes from poop held in "lagoons," or open-air holding tanks for animal waste, siphons off into water systems, creating health hazards for humans and animals living in the area.

As corporate farms moved away from the model of growing multiple crops and animals together, unique farming challenges emerged. Plants needed more fertilization, more pest control and better weed control. Petro-products provided the answer. Specially formalized petro-chemicals replaced the natural fertilizer from cows and pigs living on the integrated farms. It took a lot of the new-fangled fertilizer to feed depleted soil since crops were no longer rotated—another plus of the old model. The trees and shrubs that small farmers tended to keep as a buffer between fields were plowed under to make use of every bit of land for crops. This

loss of buffer meant more pesticides were needed to control un-
wanted bugs, because the birds and farmer-friendly insects that
ate the crop-eating insects lived in the buffering bushes. The birds
left to find foraging and shelter elsewhere, and the farmer-friendly
insects died from the pesticides along with the crop-eating ones.
As a result, our food, as Michael Pollan notes in *The Omnivore's
Dilemma*, is raised in a sea of petroleum. How can *that* be good for
us? Pesticides keep the now-free-to-enlarge populations of crop-
eating insects at bay, fertilizers push the soil to keep producing,
and herbicides control the weeds. But monoculture industrial
farms mean efficiency, and efficiency makes food cheap.

   *Obesity.* Every decade since the 1970s the United States has
witnessed a significant increase in the number of overweight and
obese children and adults. We became rather attached to the new
food, or foodlike products, as Pollan calls them in *In Defense of
Food*. New foods are developed by innovative companies every
year, and our waistlines reflect that we rather like them. Monoculture agribusiness made an extra five hundred calories of cheap
food, mostly corn, available to us each day, of which we each eat
about two hundred. In the 1960s 13 percent of the population was
obese, and now, according to the Center for Disease Control, 34
percent of Americans over twenty are obese, and 60 percent are
overweight. One in three children today has a chance of developing type 2 diabetes, and all the associated ailments of obesity.

   High fructose corn syrup is one of the culprits. It shows up in
our soft drinks (just think about how much corn syrup is in the
Big Gulp, or the Super Big Gulp!), fruit and sport drinks, Oreos,
Twizzlers, even in our granola bars and breads. We started sweet-
ening everything with corn syrup and eating more of it. While we
can't blame obesity simply on corn syrup, obesity rates did rise as
we acquired a taste for the high-fructose-corn-syrup foods that
became available for snacks and meals.

   That's some of the bad news. The silver lining is that we are capable of learning from our mistakes and are quick learners. If we choose, we can exchange cultural values of efficiency, choice and convenience for historic values rooted in connections with land and animals. People are remembering and reclaiming these values. Urban and community gardens and backyard chicken-keeping are flourishing. We are remembering other ways, besides petroleum-based fertilizers, to nurture soil, and other places, besides factory farms, to find eggs for our families. We are slowing down the process.

## FAST FOOD AND SLOW FOOD— A REVOLUTION IN EATING

Two competing social trends are vying for our loyalty. A simple barbecue joint started by Dick and Mac McDonald in 1940 became the starting place for one of them. With the unspoken motto "The Pursuit of More for Less," fast food brings us cheap, predictable and convenient food. McDonald's feeds the masses in over one hundred countries. The successful chain has been the target of books like Eric Schlosser's *Fast Food Nation* and documentaries like Morgan Spurlock's *Super Size Me* that look at the destructive, and often invisible, side of the fast-food industry. We love McDonald's, and we hate McDonald's.

Fast food is cheap and efficient, and we eat it even though we *know* that it is unhealthy. Fast food undermines values like eating dinner at home with our families, supporting our local communities, and being fair to the farm laborers and humane to the animals that provide that food for us. So while most of us still value convenience, availability, predictability, efficiency, low cost and high-volume production, we are increasingly unsettled by the unintended consequences of it all. On the other side opposing fast food is slow food, captured most literally in the Slow Food Movement.

Italy—the land of vineyards made golden in the autumn sun, and romance in the canals of Venice—is the birthplace of the Slow

Food Movement. It began in 1986 by a group of Italians affronted by the world's love affair with fast food eaten alone or while on the run. Eating a broad assortment of locally grown foods with friends while noticing and thinking about what's being eaten, where it comes from and who makes it exemplify slow food. Slow food protects historically held values about food at risk of being lost in the efficiency and growth of fast food that provides cheap, fatty, monoculture food products.

Ordinary folks wanting to take a stand against a fast-food market don't have to belong to one of the 850 worldwide Slow Food Movement chapters, or *convivium*, to create ways to celebrate food with friends. Anyone can become countercultural and may, after all, find themselves closer to a Christian view of hospitality that values relationships over efficiency. All we need is to see the goodness of slowness.

For instance, Mark and I have gathered regularly with two other families to eat shared meals in each other's homes and talk about our lives and what God is doing in them. The other two families have children in school, so negotiating schedules has been challenging at times, but we all value it enough to keep working at making it regular. Monthly we gather with another group of friends to share hearty soup-and-bread suppers in the winter, and seasonal salad suppers in the summer, as we talk about a book (usually a novel) that we've chosen to read together. We also celebrate the coming of new seasons by gathering an assortment of coworkers and friends to share food, poetry, readings and music inspired by whatever season we are leaving or heading toward. Nearly all of us have ways we can slow down and share food and friendship with others. Creating welcoming homes helps us take a breath, broaden our friendship circles and be intentional about eating.

Increasingly people taking a stand against fast food are doing so by growing some of their own food, or buying what they can from local farmers, or become small-scale farmers themselves.

## THE RETURN OF THE SMALL FAMILY FARM

Although most of the small farmers were out of business by the 1970s, their values linger still in our memories. Classics like Aldo Leopold's 1945 *Sand County Almanac* and contemporary essays of philosopher-farmer Wendell Berry have kept the ideals of the small family farm alive, along with notions of living gently and walking along *in* creation, rather than trampling *over* it. The United States is witnessing a resurgence of small family farms catering to families and communities that want to return to something local, more communal, and once again richly connected to the processes of growing, harvesting and preparing food.

These days Mark and I collect eggs from our own small flock of hens and sell the extras to my colleagues. Backyard "farming" is a growing trend across the country and we've jumped in. Last summer we built a portable coop and bought eight little chicks.

Cities across the country are responding to pressure from local residents to allow for backyard chicken-keeping. Revised ordinances spell out what will be allowed (number of hens) and what is prohibited (crowing roosters, backyard slaughtering). Many cities still prohibit backyard chickens altogether, though if neighbors don't complain some committed (or rebellious) residents raise them anyway.

Before acquiring our own brood of hens we bought our eggs from the Higgins. Mary Etta and Ed have a small family farm. Mary Etta is the primary farmer; Ed is a colleague who teaches literature and writes poetry. On Tuesdays he brings eggs to faculty lunch and I became one of his faithful buyers. I bought their eggs because I prefer to eat eggs laid by happy chickens: hens that wandered around outside eating bugs and pecking at grass, that are warmed by the sun and whose sounds comingle with neighboring birds, cows and goats. I also bought them because it was more personal than buying eggs at Thriftway. It created a social bond of sorts—I helped Ed and Mary Etta in their small farming endeavors and they gave me eggs produced locally, with minimal harm to the environment and to the hens that lay them.

*Community Supported Agriculture (CSA).* CSAs take the sort of relationship we had with the Higgins and make it more formal. They foster relationships between local farmers and the people in their communities. Individuals sign up with a local farmer and pay for a share of the harvest at the beginning of the season, and get a bag or box of produce every week throughout the growing season. We picked ours up directly from our farmers, Mike and Jill Paine, who live about seven miles away. Most subscribers pick up produce at one of a couple central drop sites arranged at the beginning of the season. We support local farmers, and they supply us with a variety of produce from early June through the end of October. Meanwhile, we support the values of the Slow Food Movement by taking the time to prepare and eat a diverse array of locally grown food. We ate our first kohlrabi, celeriac, delicata squash and fennel that summer.

*Community gardens.* By planting, tending and harvesting communal areas, neighbors are coming together to create community gardens, making their neighborhoods more beautiful and producing good food that reduces family food budgets. Community gardens get neighbors talking, laughing and working side-by-side, reflecting a form of local agriculture that has become a catalyst for neighborhood and community development. A number of New York's 744 community gardens are planted in schools where children learn the basics of gardening and eat produce they have grown. Tucson, desert town that it is, has five nationally registered community gardens and welcomes individuals and neighborhoods to start others.

A few years ago, Corey Beals, a philosophy professor at George Fox University, spearheaded an effort to get a community garden planted on our university campus. The college administrators graciously handed over an unused plot of land for the season, and a few students, staff and faculty joined Corey in creating a garden. A small concrete wading pool surrounded by sand became a central focal point, offering a play space for children while parents worked in the beds that spiraled outward and were planted with tomatoes, lavender, squash, beans, peppers, onions, mums, broccoli, basil and sunflowers. In the fall Corey and friends hosted a campuswide harvest celebration where people gathered in a tiki torch–lit garden to eat grilled food from the garden, sing and listen to local farmers talk about farming in Yamhill County. Corey expanded the garden the second year and, given the first year's success, was given more room to grow. The garden is a gift to our university community—especially to those who accept the invitation to play in the dirt and eat sun-ripened tomatoes off the vine. People who don't have space, knowledge, time or desire to manage a garden alone, but who want to busy their hands in rich, dark dirt and eat from earth's rewards later are those likely to organize or join a community garden.

Backyard gardens, CSAs and community gardens are exploding nationwide, and the values of the Slow Food Movement permeate them all. Even the White House now oversees a big vegetable garden. The first spring the Obama family took up residence in the White House, Michelle Obama brought a couple dozen children from Bancroft Elementary School to help her break ground for a garden in the South Lawn. Obama kept school children involved in the garden, which produced food for both the White House kitchen and for Miriam's Kitchen, which feeds homeless people living in D.C.

CSAs, farmers' markets and community gardens are forms of civic agriculture that take food sovereignty from global agribusinesses and return it back to local communities and farmers. But here's the rub. The takeover by agribusiness happened subtly, and mostly brought with it more choices and less expensive food. Inspiring enough people to think there is something worth taking

back can be challenging. We need convincing if supporting local
farmers means having fewer choices, *especially* if it might cost us
a bit more.

In spite of the skepticism, a civic agricultural movement is
blooming, strengthening social ties between farmers and food eaters, and boosting local economies by keeping money in our communities to be spent again. Local agriculture provides a place for
civic engagement; by supporting it, people step into their community and act neighborly.

## FOOD AND JUSTICE

During the Great Depression the government started a program to
guarantee farmers a set price for crops, helping them stay in the
food-growing business. For the sake of our country's food supply
we needed federal farm subsidies to help farmers on farms pro
duce food. Farm subsidies are a well-established and now controversial part of today's farming industry. With new subsidy transparency laws we've learned that billions of subsidy dollars go
primarily to large farming operations instead of to the farmers
trying to make a living on small and medium-sized farms. John
Peck, executive director of Family Farm Defenders, says the subsidies hurt small farmers in the United States because the rich
food corporations get big subsidies that allow them to push small
farmers out of business by selling their food for less than it costs
to grow it.

One of the Obama administration's early decisions in 2009
was to cap gross farm sales at $500,000 for a farm to be eligible
to receive subsidies (down from $750,000). While this across-
the-board cap may not be the best way to determine if the farmers who most need the subsidies receive them, it is a step toward
acknowledging that our distribution of subsidies has not bene-
fited the community of small farmers, both in the United States
and abroad.

The subsidy controversy raised questions about our ethics of global trade. The United States chose not to conform to World Trade Organization regulations that seek to make global trade fair for all countries. To conform would require eliminating our farm subsidies. Mexico offers one example for why the subsidy issue raises questions about food justice.

Mexican farmers can grow corn for less than U.S. farmers can, but federal subsidies allow large corporate farms to sell their corn on the world market (including in Mexico) for much less than it costs U.S. farmers to grow it, underselling the Mexican farmers. Since the establishment of the North American Free Trade Agreement (NAFTA) in 1994, 1.3 million Mexican farmers have lost their livelihood. These farmers can no longer make a living for their families on their farms so they move to cities to work in factories, or become migrant laborers.

When is food "just food"? What does it mean to extend justice in matters of farming? Do we have a responsibility to be global citizens and to extend fairness beyond our borders? These questions are being raised in national and international conversations. We are more able to be agents of God's desire for justice in the world if we reflect on these questions in light of our faith. If the prophet Isaiah were here, he might pull out his message to Israel as recorded in Isaiah 58. The Israelites were fasting and praying, seeking healing and forgiveness, and wondering why God did not seem to notice. God says:

> I will tell you why! . . .
> It's because you are fasting to please yourselves.
> Even while you fast,
>     you keep oppressing your workers. . . .
> No, this is the kind of fasting I want:
> Free those who are wrongly imprisoned;
>     lighten the burden of those who work for you.

Let the oppressed go free,
    and remove the chains that bind people.
Share your food with the hungry,
    and give shelter to the homeless.
Give clothes to those who need them,
    and do not hide from relatives who need your help.
Then your salvation will come like the dawn,
    and your wounds will quickly heal.
Your godliness will lead you forward,
    and the glory of the LORD will protect you from behind.
Then when you call, the LORD will answer.
    "Yes, I am here," he will quickly reply. (Isaiah 58:3, 6-9)

First, to extend justice I have to acknowledge that I *have* neighbors—men, women and children whose work, after all, supplies me with food. My neighbors include the field laborers, ranchers, and dairy, cannery, factory and slaughterhouse workers who grow or process my food. Acknowledging that real people spend their lives being sure I get fed removes the veil that allows all those people, animals and unsavory processes to stay comfortably invisible.

Invisibility encourages me to purchase inexpensive, highly subsidized food and feel like I am being a *responsible* shopper because I'm getting the most for my money. But when I truly see my neighbors—the Honduran farmer trying to get a fair price for his bananas; the small U.S. family trying to make a living farming in sustainable ways that are good for the soil, the insects, the critters sharing the land and the people consuming the food; subsistence farmers in South America who lose access to land they have lived off for generations, land taken away and planted in corn sent to feedlots to fatten cows I'll eat—I become a responsible shopper by eating in ways that reflect justice, fairness and ecological health for all God's creation.

To extend justice to our neighbors, our brothers and sisters, our fellow humans, is to protect their livelihoods and to stop contributing to their oppression through our desire for inexpensive chocolate, beef and corn. Food justice cannot happen if my inexpensive food undermines another's ability to feed, clothe and educate their children.

Therefore, loving my neighbor means examining my food habits, including my assumption that being a responsible shopper means stretching our family's food dollar as far as possible. This is the focus of the next chapter—what it looks like to eat with intention and to dine at tables of compassion. For some of us, loving our neighbor will include learning about these bigger pieces, perhaps researching farm subsidies, and encouraging senators and representatives to support farm bills that come before Congress every few years in an attempt to reform subsidy laws that give the advantage to the special interests of agribusiness.

## A QUESTION OF CLASS

Before I could address what a compassionate table might look like, I had to wrestle with a question related to social class. I want to walk gently in my food choices, but a complex piece of the conversation is related to issues of politics, privilege and class. Can lower-class families afford to be mindful of neighbors here and abroad who provide them with less expensive food?

At some point it dawned on me, a sociologist who is concerned about social inequality, that buying fair-trade coffee and cocoa, hormone-free and antibiotic-free milk, and eggs from Ed and Mary Etta's "happy" chickens is possible because I'm comfortably situated in the upper-middle class. When Mark and I first married we were both still in college and therefore qualified as members of the lower class, although we had good potential for moving up. During Mark's graduate-school days we went grocery shopping holding a daughter with one hand and clipped coupons with the other.

We couldn't afford grapes or broccoli and shopped for bargains. My focus in those days was stretching our dollars to feed our growing family. Working-class and lower-class families today confront the same challenges we did thirty years ago.

Several significant issues are wrapped into the question, can the lower class eat with intention toward issues of fairness and justice? One is the availability and affordability of just food for people in the lower class. If I live in an urban city's low-income housing and am dependent on public transportation, my closest grocer will supply me with my food. Even if I wanted to, I wouldn't have options to buy eggs from "happy" chickens, or fairly traded coffee and cocoa. If I live on a low income, Walmart allows my household budget dollars to go further than they would go at Whole Foods. Convenient, inexpensive food is an asset in my life, and in a life without many assets, I take what I can get.

This question of food justice is part of a larger conversation about social justice. It can be seen in the difference between the annual income of large winery owners in Yamhill County and the hourly pay of the Hispanic laborers working in their vineyards, or between the net worth of the owners of Walmart and the wages received by employees of any given Walmart. Fighting for food justice is part of a larger fight for change in social, economic and political structures that contribute to the widening gap between the wealthy and the poor. It means asking hard questions like: What does it say about us as a country when citizens that work full time still fall below the poverty line, earning less than what the government computes is necessary to stay out of poverty? What is my responsibility to work for change in a system that requires some citizens to choose between going to the doctor and paying their electric bill?

But yes, there are ways that lower-class families can attend to issues of justice in their food choices. The summer of 2009 saw an explosion of urban community gardens in response to an uncertain economy. Vacant lots in low-income metropolitan areas are now full of fruits and vegetables, making it possible for residents to stretch their grocery dollars with free fresh produce. My hope is that after the economy recovers, the gardens will stay.

Mike and Jill Paine donate 10 percent of their CSA shares to "food insecure families," low-income families who couldn't otherwise afford to receive the bounty we get from an Oregon harvest. Other shareholders can make a donation as well, but whether or not we do, Mike and Jill are committed to being sure some of their bounty goes to low-income families in our community. In some cities and towns in the United States, community food banks open to low-income citizens receive fresh produce donations from CSAs and other community gardens.

If low-income families are supported by the Supplemental Nutrition Assistance Program, they can use the assistance they receive at grocers that carry whole foods, organic, hormone- and antibiotic-free products, and fairly traded products and produce. The support will not go as far, so families will have to be more selective in their food choices, but it does give them some degree of freedom to select just food.

Food justice for those of us in the middle class is more a matter of *will* than of *means*. It's getting beyond an entrenched virtue of frugality that says we are *more* responsible as a shopper when we shop for bargains. We feel, as Barbara Kingsolver notes in *Animal, Vegetable, Miracle*, a compulsion to economize on food. Yet this compulsion rarely spills over into other places in our lives. Kingsolver says,

> The majority of Americans buy bottled drinking water, for example, even though water runs from the faucets at home for a fraction of the cost, and government quality standards are stricter for tap water than for bottled. At any income level, we can be relied upon for categorically unnecessary

purchases . . . name-brand clothing instead of plainer gear. "Economizing," as applied to clothing, generally means looking for discount name brands instead of wearing last year's clothes again. The dread of rearing unfashionable children is understandable. But as a priority, "makes me look cool" has passed up "keeps arteries functional" and left the kids huffing and puffing (fashionably) in the dust.

Spending more on food for the health of our children motivates a lot of us. Spending more on food for the health and well-being of others could motivate us as well, reflecting our Christian call for compassion and justice. Instead of thinking that paying ninety-nine cents a pound for fairly traded bananas, or three to four dollars for a dozen eggs from hens free to scratch in a barnyard and hunt for bugs and sunshine, is a scandalous extravagance, we could begin to think it scandalous *not* to consider the well-being and lives of people and animals who provide us with food. We make multiple food choices every week; perhaps we would be more inclined to make "just" decisions over frugal ones if we saw it as a Christian value to do so.

Sometimes the middle class turns ethical eating into a class issue because we feel paralyzed by what we don't know about food. The night the class that met at my home talked about food, students said they had neither money nor time to eat "organic," which for them meant eating just about any whole food—a potato, for instance, or a green bean. Their only perceived option was to buy frozen pizza or boxed macaroni and cheese. I don't fault them. They are a product of a brand of entrepreneurial agribusiness that promised to give us cheap food, and already prepared. They can hardly imagine anything different.

But the conversation is turning, and imaginative ideas about food offer pathways out of feeling stuck. George Fox University hosted "Food Meet 2010" and invited local farmers, food producers and food activists to meet with interested folks in the community to talk about food, including how to make eating simply and locally affordable and practical for low-income families. We had standing-room only in the auditorium where we watched and discussed a few clips from the documentary *Food, Inc.*, and a high-energy bustle around the vendor tables suggested inspiring change is underway.

## CONCLUSION

Except for a few staples, and the bushels of apples, pears and peaches that Grandpa would drive over to eastern Colorado to buy each fall, the food Grandma fed my mother and her siblings in the 1930s and 1940s mostly came from the family garden and the farm. Aunt Geri and Uncle Bill took over the farm eventually, and my cousin Bill and his wife, Sharon, farmed it after them. They hung on to it longer than many family farmers in their generation, yet sold it in 2001 to someone who bought up a number of farms in the area.

In two generations we arrived at a place where most people in the United States didn't think much about locally produced food, and would have struggled to find it if they did. But family farms are making a comeback, and CSAs, urban gardens and community gardens are giving people opportunities to support local farmers and to be minifarmers themselves. Besides that inspiring change, small businesses have begun partnering with local farmers around the world, offering farmers in the Global South fair prices for coffee, cocoa, teas and tropical fruits.

In this global food economy how you eat impacts families in Uganda and Guatemala and farmers in Illinois and California. How you eat impacts land, water, bugs and birds. To walk gently means eating compassionately and justly—in ways that are sustainable for the land—and fostering the well-being of God's people and creation.

o o o

## RESOURCES

*Where can I learn about U-Pick places near me?*

- www.pickyourown.org/index.htm
  This site has all kinds of information about finding farms near you, planting, harvesting, food storage tips. The site is a community effort as individuals keep the information updated for the site.

*How can I learn more about farm subsidies?*

- International Debate Education Association (IDEA) develops, organizes and promotes debate and debate-related activities in communities throughout the world. The following link offers a good pro/con summary of farm subsidies: www.idebate.org/debatabase/ topic_details.php?topicID=613.
  *400 West 59th Street*
  *New York, NY 10019*

*Where can I learn about the chocolate and coffee trades?*

- The International Labor Rights Forum (ILRF) is an advocacy organization dedicated to achieving just and humane treatment for workers worldwide. The ILRF follows a number of industries with labor abuses. See the link for a specific look at the cocoa trade: www .laborrights.org/stop-child-labor/cocoa-campaign.
  *2001 S. St. NW #420*
  *Washington, D.C. 20009*
  *Phone: (202) 347-4100*

- Off, Carol. *Bitter Chocolate: Investigating the Dark Side of the World's Most Seductive Sweet.* Toronto: Random House Canada, 2006. This book sounds an alarm about the cocoa industry and raises awareness.

- *UN Chronicle Online* is the magazine for the United Nations, covering issues being taken up by the UN. The following link is specific to the coffee trade and its Millennium Development Goals ramifications: www.un.org/Pubs/chronicle/2007/webArticles/111407_coffee_trade.html.

*DC1 900A, United Nations*
*New York, NY 10017*

- The documentary *Black Gold* (prod. and dir. Marc Francis and Nick Francis, 78 min., Fulcrum Productions, 2007) is an exposé of the multibillion-dollar coffee industry and the fight for a fair price for farmers. See <www.blackgoldmovie.com> for more information.

*How can I learn more about animal rights issues and legislation?*

- For ongoing updates on legislation: http://sourcewatch.org/index.php?title=U.S._animal_rights_legislation.

- Not One Sparrow offers a Christian perspective on animal rights and animal care: http://notonesparrow.com.

- The Humane Society of the United States. Their extensive website offers background information on an assortment of animal-related issues plus updates on legislation and ways to act. The following link below is specific to farm animals: www.hsus.org/farm/.

*2100 L Street, NW*
*Washington, D.C. 20037*
*Phone: (202) 452-1100*

## FURTHER READING AND DOCUMENTARY SUGGESTIONS

*Where can I go to find out about older food cultures and regional U.S. food cultures?*

- D'Aluisio, Faith, and Peter Menzel. *What the World Eats.* Berkeley, Calif.: Tricycle Press, 2008. A great exploration of the variety of foods around the world through photo journalism, tables and charts. Great for any age.

- Klindienst, Patricia. *The Earth Knows My Name: Food, Culture, and Sustainability in the Gardens of Ethnic America.* Boston: Beacon Press, 2007.

- For Indian food: www.food-india.com/.

- For African food: www.africaguide.com/cooking.htm.

- For U.S. food culture check out Linda Stradley's website What's Cooking America: www.whatscookingamerica.net.

- For an overview of the "New American Food Culture," read John Ikerd's article. Ikerd is Professor Emeritus of Agricultural Economics at the University of Missouri: www.kerrcenter.com/nws ltr/2005/spring2005/food_culture.htm.

- *Food, Inc.* (prod. and dir. Robert Kenner and Eric Scholosser, 93 min., Magnolia Pictures, 2009). Filmmaker Robert Kenner pulls back the curtain that keeps our food industry largely invisible and shows viewers what they need to see to be more informed food consumers.

- *King Corn* (dir. Aaron Wolf, 88 min., Mosaic Films, 2007). Director Aaron Wolf follows two college friends on an eleven-month journey to track the story of corn—how it is grown and where it goes. Author Michael Pollan assists them along the way.

# PRELUDE

## Help Me, and Let Me Help You

*Boa Me Na Me Mmoa Wo*

Reading 1 John has been like a slap in the face. I first encountered its severity while attending Wheaton College. One particular spring morning I headed over to the dining hall, Bible and journal in hand, for my typical morning routine where I'd enjoy a relaxed breakfast of reading and contemplating. I went to Sang, the chef who made my morning omelet, then sat down at my favorite table, huddled against the window where I could bask in the sun, and began reading 1 John.

> We must not be like Cain who was from the evil one and murdered his brother. . . . We know that we have passed from death to life because we love one another. Whoever does not love abides in death. . . . We know love by this, that he laid down his life for us—and we ought to lay down our lives for one another. How does God's love abide in anyone who has the world's goods and sees a brother or sister in need and yet refuses help?

Little children, let us love, not in word or speech, but in truth and action. (1 John 3:12-18 NRSV)

As I read, it began to take on new meaning. Being the faithful sociology student that I was I decided to take a social and economic lens to it. Once I opened this lens to the text I became angry and frustrated. How could God demand so much of me, how could I consistently act in love when I lived in a world where so often social structures and economic systems are built by Cain and run off of the blood of Abel? As I sat in my comfortable chair eating my omelet, contemplating love, my mind drifted to Sang, who is a refugee from Vietnam living and working in the United States. Beyond the face-to-face encounter, how could *I* love her? My focus shifted from Sang to my plate. Where did the eggs for my omelet come from? Were the hens treated humanely? And the vegetables—were farmers given a fair price for them? I moved from my omelet to my clothes. My clothes, oh my clothes—the skirt I was wearing, yup, made in India, the shoes, the cell phone, it didn't stop.

As I sat there my anger turned to grief. How could I love my neighbors when I am enmeshed in social structures that so often are not structures of love, and do not contribute to life? What does that look like in this globalized world when the benefits I receive (cheap groceries, clothes and access to a million choices) come at cost to another? *How could I stop being Cain in the implicit decisions required of me day to day?* How could I retrain myself to listen to Abel's cry and respond? These were the questions that began to haunt me as a student at Wheaton College. And they haunt me still.

I decided to focus on one area of my life. I wasn't sure I was quite ready to investigate the gritty reality of where my beloved dresses came from, or give up my leisurely transportation, so I began with my diet. I usually eat three times a day, which is twenty-one meals a week, and *that* is a lot of food. A lot of food equals a large impact. An impact that could either be life-giving to local communities or cause further harm and violence. I've struggled to translate compassion and love onto my plate and into my coffee mug. How do I have compassion for the cocoa and coffee farmers in the way I consume my mochas? If I'm honest, sometimes my mochas are contributing to their well-being, but more often, I benefit from the low cost of cocoa and coffee.

In the summer of 2007 I did one of my seminary internships at the Church of Christ in Ghana, and while I was there I was able to learn a lot about Ghanaian history, traditional culture and some of their current agriculture. My friends Eugene and Dio took me to a local cocoa farm where I was able to see what cocoa looks like before it is delivered neatly into my mochas. Did you know it grows on trees? It is quite a magnificent and complicated process, and one that could bring a lot of income into Ghana. Unfortunately, most Ghanaian farmers are not receiving much of the profit from their cocoa farms. They often sell their cocoa to the multinational corporations like Nestlé that have the power to set the price and set it so low that once the cocoa is formulated into a chocolate bar, it's so expensive that the cocoa farmer can't afford it! Cocoa and coffee farmers in Ethiopia, Kenya, Ivory Coast and many other countries experience the same.

The compassionate table isn't supposed to be comprised of a massive, guilt-ridden to-do list. I often find it an adventurous challenge: how to sustain my body in a compassionate way. When I engage this challenge, I find that I actually enjoy my food more. One of the amazing things about changing my diet to eat lower on the food chain is that it has helped me to become conscious in other ways. Eating takes up a lot of our time and energy, so it serves as a constant reminder that I am striving to live a compassionate and loving life, striving to be on the side of Abel, saying no to the systems and structures that Cain established. This reminder given to me in the form of food helps me to look at other aspects of my life in the same light.

The apostle John is clear about the fact that we are to be *in the light,* to be sources of life, to love, to *lay down our lives* for our brothers and sisters. But how do we do this in a complex world where so many of our daily decisions make us complicit in other people's suffering? How do we as a community move in a way that supports life, a way in which we love neighbors whom we cannot see? How do we lay down our lives in the mundane decisions that don't even feel like moral decisions, like what we cook and where we shop for groceries? The temptation is to turn this into one more giant checklist for moral living. But instead, this can be a process of asking how we can be creative and life-giving in our everyday lives. How can we find true, full and abundant life? The Ghanaian symbol *Boa Me Na Me Mmoa Wo* means, "Help me, and let me help you," symbolizing the need for cooperation and our innate interdependence. We need to help one another, and we need to allow others to help us. Our actions in our farms, in grocery stores, in kitchens and on our plates affect one another. Part of finding abundant life is discovering how and where we are interconnected and how and where we may help our neighbors near and far.

It sounds silly, I know, but when I wear my ecofriendly shoes, or my fair-trade dress, or cook a plant-based meal made with local ingredients, I enjoy them more. I savor the fullness of these gifts. I never knew how much I could enjoy food, or shoes, for that matter. It's not about guilt; it is about enjoyment and deep satisfaction. Knowing that these decisions contribute to good, contribute to life and light in the world. This is not only abundant living for others, but for ourselves too. It is the satisfaction of living well, of being beacons of light and life.

# DINING AT TABLES
# OF COMPASSION

*All sorrows are less with bread.*

—MIGUEL DE CERVANTES, *DON QUIXOTE*

Susan and her daughter Meghan move with grace-filled gentleness, serving food and preparing and pouring our teas. It is my fiftieth birthday and I am celebrating with women who have known me long and deep. We sit in our dining room with the sounds and smells of a June day bursting in through open windows. The table is set with my mother-in-law's Spode Camilla Pink dishes she loaned me for the occasion, and my daughter Rae's vase of pink peonies add charm to the old-fashioned look of the table. We are drinking a variety of teas and eating Susan's scones, olive and cucumber sandwiches, a tomato and pepper sauce on polenta, mushroom-filled zucchini boats and strawberries dipped in dark chocolate. These dear women, my mother-in-law, sister-in-law, three daughters, a niece and four friends, each tell a story—with me and the storyteller of the moment as the main characters. I am moved and blessed by the stories they tell, what they remember and select out of all the possibilities. Real food, deep friends, shared history. I savor the memory of it.

When we celebrate life as we savor food, we hold together God's sustaining abundance and the cry and hope for justice in the world. We celebrate lives of hope with laughter, even as we acknowledge that all is not right—in our own lives, and in the world. Celebrating with just food tangibly acknowledges that while the world has significant troubles, hope bursts forth in food that bountifully blooms and grows year after year. God is sustaining us. Eating justly is a profoundly simple act that recognizes that God's goodness and a call for justice comingle on our plates.

Just food throws gladness back at God who made us creative creatures. Humans figured out how to distill Pinot Noir and Riesling wines from grapes and how to make Gouda and Havarti cheeses from goat and cow milk. We make bread, naan, tortillas and pasta using an assortment of grains and can roast vegetables, make fruit pies, dry tomatoes and spices, or eat all of these raw and fresh. We combine all sorts of foods into magnificent dishes, not simply to satisfy our hunger but also to tease our palates with taste and texture. How grateful I am not to be a cow that simply eats grass, or our cat Mrs. Pollifax, who prefers raw mice to black bean and sweet potato enchiladas! To kiss our fingertips and say, "voilá!" is to say, Thank you, God, for the marvelous raw materials you made available, the creativity you endowed us with to figure out what to do with it all and the taste buds to enjoy it!

But we are caught up in something of a paradox, as described in chapter two. Food is magnificent, an amazing blessing of God's creation, yet our eating habits have ethical dimensions, and loving our neighbor requires us to eat intentionally. Eating with intention embraces pleasure and celebrates good food while being mindful of and attending to our obligation to others, to God's creatures and to earth.

As you read the last chapter, perhaps you felt compelled to act by the concerns I raised but found yourself asking what can be done about it. How can I truly love my neighbor in this complex, global food economy? In this chapter I offer four principles for dining at tables of compassion, and describe various examples of how you can do this as you make everyday food choices.

## PRINCIPLE 1: EAT LOCALLY

The century-old phrase "think global, act local" has become standard bumper sticker fare in the last two decades. This phrase captures my first two principles, although I have reversed the order and changed the wording a bit.

We choose the recipients of our food dollars. We give some of them to the General Mills' CEO, some to the Del Monte production managers, the PepsiCo sales managers, advertising companies that entice us to buy Fritos and Betty Crocker cake mixes, and check-out clerks at our grocery stores. With each choice we support different food industries as we buy our food. When we buy local produce and products at farmers' markets we are supporting the livelihoods of farmers in our neighborhood, as almost all of the money we spend goes back to the farmer. Besides being good for the farmer, when we buy local we forge relationships based on interdependence and build our sense of belonging, diminishing the isolation we've grown accustomed to with all our autonomy and choice.

Buying local means we also indirectly support local farmers worldwide by freeing up farmers in places like Ecuador to plant and sell food for their own neighbors, instead of for us. Global trade, like buying bananas from Ecuador, *can* be good for local economies, but not when trade practices undermine the food security of people in Ecuadorian villages. Our desire for inexpensive products that can only grow near the equator compromises food security for people who spend their best energy and soil supplying us with bananas, coffee, mangos and pineapple rather than growing the produce necessary for their own people to eat well.

The more I have learned about agribusiness, monoculture farming and issues of global trade, the more I have tried to find local sources of food. Some people have approached this with great zeal, such as Barbara Kingsolver and her family, who committed to eating all local foods for a year. Each family member chose one exception. Mark and I had a conversation about what our exceptions would be (chocolate for Mark, coffee for me so long as he shared his chocolate), but we haven't mustered the resolve to take this beyond the hypothetical. Still, there are daily decisions we can all make to shop more locally.

*Consider giving up one non-local food and adding a local one.* Every decision exercises our power to choose thoughtfully. Giving up one non-local food may mean giving up maple syrup shipped from the east coast if you live on the west coast, or oranges brought from California or Florida if you live in the north. Adding a local food could be as simple as buying cheese and ice cream from a local dairy, instead of from cows living in Wisconsin (unless you are *from* Wisconsin). If you are from Oregon it could mean buying hazelnuts and walnuts instead of pecans and almonds. In general, notice where your food comes from, and buy food grown or produced close to home.

*Shop at farmers' markets or CSAs.* It's not just folks living in rural America surrounded by farms who can support local farmers anymore. Farmers' markets and CSAs are becoming commonplace in small towns, the suburbs and urban centers such as New York, Detroit and Tucson. More of us have access to locally grown produce.

*Grow your own food.* The most local any of us can get is to eat from our own yards. Most of us don't have the time or interest for big gardens, but I get the impression people lack confidence more than they lack time. They aren't sure they could get spinach or corn seeds or a spindly tomato plant to actually grow something edible. Perhaps we have a crisis of confidence because fewer of us grew up with backyard gardens than our parents did. Despite this we're seeing a flourishing of green as gardens take root in urban and suburban neighborhoods. From tomatoes and herbs in patio pots to community gardens filling vacant lots, people are gaining confidence as they watch seeds turn into food.

Celebrating the wonder of food comes rather automatically when you watch seeds open, unfolding themselves as they crack the soil, stretching skinny stalks toward the sky. Just weeks later they pop out blossoms that become beans, acorn squash or cantaloupe. Seeds know what to do without coaching; gardening is humbling in that way. We don't actually have much to do with growing food except creating a space for seeds to germinate and grow, watering them occasionally, knocking down a few weeds (which appears to be somewhat optional), and then harvesting the bounty that comes. Thankfulness and wonder wash over me every summer—an annual gratitude from knowing I am eating well, and in ways that work with seasonal cycles and multiple interdependent relationships found throughout God's creation.

## PRINCIPLE 2: THINK GLOBALLY

The Hebrew noun *shalom* describes a peace that prevails because justice reigns; the world is set right. *Shalom* includes universal flourishing, wholeness, the perfection of God's creation, prosperity and peace. And so, as we pause to say grace at our tables—and what a grace it is to be blessed with foods that delight us—we can also be mindful of a world that groans for redemption and can pray for hearts that will pursue justice and seek *shalom*.

*See the world as it is.* Justice involves seeing the world as a place of beauty and potential as well as exploitation and sorrow—and then acting rightly and compassionately in response. Justice is the foundation upon which other virtues rest; a hope for peace that prevails because the world is right is why we seek wisdom, shore up courage to do right and live in moderation. Pursuing justice requires us to see and empathize with the daily lives of others around the world. This means we will not shield ourselves from the reality that eight hundred million chronically malnourished people share this planet with us. We will not turn away from the suffering of human trafficking where women and children are kidnapped, deceived and sold into the horrific sex trade or sold as slave laborers in the coffee, cocoa and cotton industries in West Africa. Even sweatshops that provide paid employment for women and children in the Global South do so without giving them basic rights you and I take for granted. You can probably stay home if you are sick without fear of losing your job, and you are probably paid overtime if you are required to work it. You can get up and go to the bathroom during the day when you need to, and you are probably protected from work-related hazards, or given protection if you have to work around chemicals or dangerous equipment. Even if you are working a minimum-wage job, if you work fifty to seventy hours a week as most sweatshop workers do, you will probably make enough to feed your family.

Seeking justice means we will learn something about the global trade conversation *intending for the knowing to impact our choices* and hoping it will inspire us to find one issue that we are particularly passionate about and join others fighting for justice. You may end up writing letters to your local representatives, grocers or international apparel and chocolate companies, writing editorials for local papers, or speaking of these matters in your church. If that sounds overwhelming to you (and it would to me), know that the starting place is simply a willingness to see that the world is *not* a place where everyone's life is mostly like yours, even when it comes to something as basic as access to food.

At the June 2008 World Summit in Rome the UN secretary general Ban Ki-moon said, "The rapidly escalating crisis of food availability around the world has reached emergency proportions." In the prior three years the price of basics like wheat, corn and rice doubled. The world is paying close attention to such matters since the establishment of the Millennium Development Goals (MDGs) at the beginning of the twenty-first century. This unprecedented effort by the United Nations to coordinate a global community push to halve extreme poverty and end hunger by 2015 ignited supportive movements around the world. Organizations mobilized to help make it happen, like ONE, a U.S.-based organization working to address AIDS and extreme poverty, and the Micah Challenge, an international Christian organization dedicated to eradicating poverty in the poorest countries of the world.

Most of the MDGs showed encouraging progress in the first nine years of the campaign. Yet World Bank president Robert Zoellick estimates that global food shortages could set the world back seven years in the fight against extreme poverty and global disease. The Food and Agriculture Organization's solution is for wealthy countries to assist countries with hungry populations to grow more food, which is a better response than *sending* food. Sending food aid directly is only a partial answer because it contributes to the larger problem of poverty by undermining local farmers' ability to sell crops in their own communities. Besides undermining local farmers, food aid increases dependence on other countries for food. To end long-term hunger, giving food needs to be matched with investing in agricultural development— including infrastructure; better access to water, seeds and tools; and fighting for fair-trade practices and against economic and political policies that undermine a village or country's efforts to feed its own people.

When Jason Fileta, coordinator of Micah Challenge USA, talked with Micah Challenge directors from Africa, the top priority they voiced for what needed to happen for the MDGs to be realized was reforming international trade practices. This took priority over assistance through foreign aid or debt relief. A similar problem that U.S. farm subsidies present to Mexican farmers (discussed in the last chapter) affects trade in Africa. Subsidies paid to U.S. agribusiness allow them to undersell African farmers, particularly when trade deals negotiated with the United States require many African nations to eliminate tariffs on U.S. imports as a way to encourage trade in Africa. However, we continue to place tariffs on African goods we import, making it difficult for African products to compete either in the U.S. market or in Africa. My sense is that for the most part the right hand (export trade) doesn't know what the left hand (import trade) is doing—at least I have to hope so; otherwise trade practices seem downright evil. Maybe they are. Regardless, the double whammy is crippling for a continent attempting to engage global trade and alleviate poverty for its people.

*Buy global food from sources that use fair-trade practices.* The effect of U.S. farm subsidies on Mexican and African farmers provides one example of a food justice issue; foods grown near the equator offer another. Coffee and cocoa and tropical fruits like bananas and pineapples need year-round warmth to grow well. Because farmers near the equator are neither wealthy nor powerful, they are vulnerable to international practices that compromise the well-being of local area farmers, families and communities.

Multinational corporations (MNCs) like Dole, Nestlé, Folgers and Del Monte went south and established plantations and/or gained control of those markets at a substantial profit. Most coffee farmers in Kenya sell their beans at the auction through one of three recognized marketing agents, receiving about nine cents for a pound of coffee beans. That same pound of Kenyan coffee can be bought for about nine dollars at a coffee shop or a grocery store, or turn a significant profit at a Java Joe's drive-through via mochas, cappuccinos and the coffee of the day. There is money to be made in the coffee business—but not by the farmers taking care of the fields and producing the beans. At first it seemed like a good idea to get the Global North addicted to caffeine. Countries at the equator were guaranteed a market for their goods, and we got to enjoy exotic coffees at affordable prices. But since the late 1970s when the coffee trade boomed, earnings for coffee farmers have dwindled while earnings for those running the transactions have escalated. Small coffee farmers can no longer feed their families on the profits, or afford to buy the uniforms necessary to send their children to the public school. Advocating for fair trade and combating unfair trade practices at the political level is one way we can work toward justice. Shopping fair trade is another.

When we purchase coffee where the relationship with the farmer who grows and harvests coffee beans is respectable and fair, coffee tastes better. If a coffee shop has a relationship with a farmer, or sells fair-trade coffee, the owner usually advertises it. If you don't see any telltale signage, then ask the barista, and if she or he doesn't know, ask them to find out. By asking you are letting the coffee shop owner know that you are looking to buy coffee that supports the communities from which it comes. The more customers ask, the more likely it is that coffee shop owners will look into making fair-trade coffee available.

A clear conscience is good for the taste buds. And when the beans are grown in their natural habitat—in the shade under a canopy of trees instead of in plowed fields in the sun where they need to be fed with fertilizers—we can savor our coffee knowing we are fostering greater justice for farmers and greater ecological care for creation.

*Trust the fair-trade label.* Fair-trade products do carry a higher price tag. If you are like me, you want to know what purchasing them accomplishes, especially if you are given to skepticism about companies' marketing ploys, which can make us *think* we are buying labor-friendly and earth-friendly products when we really aren't. How can we know for sure that coffee has been fairly traded and that the money we spend contributes to the community's well-being?

Fair-trade certification was established to create social and en-

vironmental standards for international companies, evidence
that trade can be a path for sustainable development in the Global
South. The certification "Fair Trade" means just that—trade that
is just and fair. It brings the benefits of international trade into
the hands of people and communities that most need it. Rather
than the profit going to an MNC that sets up business in Honduras or Ghana, the profit stays in the community where food is
grown and harvested.

Fair-trade practices benefit individuals around the world who
receive reliable work at a fair and livable wage. Fair trade also
seeks to alleviate unjust labor practices that keep communities in
poverty and dependent on foreigners to set up factories and farms
in their cities and countryside. The goal is to free people economically to feed themselves and their children, to improve their overall health, and to release their children to go to school, rather than
having to send them to work in fields or factories.

The surest way to know you are buying fair-trade products is to
purchase products with the fair-trade mark. But getting the fair-
trade certification is costly, and some conscientious storeowners
can't find enough customers willing to pay more for fairly traded
goods. Starbucks currently offers fair-trade coffee for people wanting to support just food practices, and regular (not fair-trade) coffee for those who don't.

*Look for direct-trade products and practices.* Coffees, teas,
spices, clothes, baskets, jewelry and other imported goods don't
have to be certified fair trade (or organic for that matter) to be fair
trade and/or organic. Some conscientious coffee bean buyers, coffee shops and retailers bypass fair-trade certification and set up
direct relationships with local farmers in the Global South, and
then maintain transparency so anyone can hold them accountable
for their business dealings. Stumptown Coffee Roasters, a Portland, Oregon, based coffee company, is one example. Stumptown
has a direct relationship with farmers in Central and South Amer-

ica, Africa and Indonesia. The company is committed to supporting farmers who are also committed to the well-being of their field
laborers, and to farming in sustainable ways that are mindful of
the land and water. The company pays fair or above fair prices for
their coffee. Intentionally looking for and purchasing direct-trade
and fair-trade products helps us support and remember people
around the world working hard to feed their families, particularly
now in the face of the global food crisis.

Thinking globally and staying mindful of a global food crisis is
more challenging when food is abundant for us. The fact is, except
for paying a bit more for food, most of us won't feel the food crisis.
Sure, we drove a bit less when gas prices climbed beyond four dollars per gallon in 2008, and we started driving smaller cars, but
most of us can pay the additional dollars required for gas at the
pump and food on the grocery-store shelf. But food security has
been compromised for lower-class families in our own country,
and severely so for people in the Global South. Dr. Diouf, the UN
Food and Agriculture Organization director, said that the crisis
already had "tragic political and social consequences" in terms of
world peace and security. "The problem of food insecurity is a
political one. It is a question of priorities in the face of the most
fundamental of human needs."

In the summer of 2008 eight of the wealthiest countries in the
world (known as the G-8) met in Japan to address hunger and
starvation. Leaders around the world see a hunger crisis that is
not going away easily or soon, and the ministers of agriculture
from the G-8 countries are working on strategies to combat global
agricultural and food security issues. Even with the global economic crisis that affects the G-8 countries, the hunger crisis continues to be a high-priority agenda item. However uncomfortable
hunger is to talk about, or however difficult it is to agree on a plan
to combat it, addressing hunger is fundamental to loving our
neighbors. A starting place is to mostly shop locally, but do so

with an eye on the world, thinking globally and buying from the
Global South when you can do so in ways that support local communities elsewhere.

## PRINCIPLE 3: AVOID FOOD TAINTED
## WITH MISERY

Does God desire justice for animals too? For the 280 million hens
laying our eggs at any given time? For the cows and pigs that give
us hamburger and bacon?

Maybe courage means lifting our veil of ignorance and learning
how factory farms, feedlots and slaughterhouses do the business
of fattening and slaughtering animals for our tables. Perhaps after
exploring the issues we'd join the growing number of people making a difference with their votes, like Californians who worked
toward legislation to fight for fair treatment of animals in animal
industries—including the banning of battery cages. Proposition
2, the Prevention of Farm Animal Cruelty Act, passed in November 2008 and included preventing animal cruelty, supporting family farmers and other common-sense reforms. California is the
fifth largest egg-producing state, so the bill will affect a lot of hens.
We can all become informed consumers and join efforts that extend our compassion to animals.

Animals are first and foremost God's living creatures. They are
not primarily ours. Animals breathe, bask, sleep, eat and suffer in
community with us. They birth and raise their young, try to stay
alive when threatened, experience fear and pain, pleasure and
well-being. In these ways we are not so dissimilar. But humans are
the species with the most capacity to manipulate aspects of creation, which is what allows us to also be garden tenders, animal
keepers, miners, teachers, developers and builders. All that extra
stuff we can do to manipulate the environment means domesticated and wild animals depend on us to varying degrees to keep
their lives tolerable. Since they need many of the same things we

do—sun, good water, clean air and fertile soil—their ability to relish in the abundance of a healthy planet and in having space to do the creaturely things God hard-wired in them to do is dependent on us. In this day of corporate farming and feedlots it takes courage and fortitude to treat animals respectfully, protecting their creaturely lives even as we use them for our own ends.

Switzerland, Germany, Sweden and Austria have all decided that justice should be extended to animals that provide us with nourishment and have banned wire battery cages in their countries. And, though many of the examples in chapter two cast corporations in a negative light, there are positive things happening in the corporate world. While the United States allows wire battery cages, a number of companies and stores have taken a stand against them.

Fedele Bauccio, the CEO of Bon Appétit Management Company, took the risk to be a socially responsible company in a competitive food-service market. Bon Appétit's mission is to provide food services for a sustainable future to more than four hundred U.S. schools and corporations. In 1999 the Farm to Fork program began, using produce from local farmers rather than from corporations. In 2005 Bon Appétit implemented the cage-free egg policy, making the costly choice to use eggs from chickens that were treated more humanely.

Bon Appétit is not the only company with a conscience. Burgerville, Finagle a Bagel and Wolfgang Puck no longer use caged eggs. Burger King, Denny's, Carl's Jr. and Hardee's have started to move away from caged eggs. Hotel chains, like Omni Hotels, will not serve battery caged eggs at any of their 40 hotels, and over 350 schools and universities have eliminated or significantly reduced their use of eggs from hens housed in battery cages.

Those of us who do the grocery shopping for our families have choices too. Whole Foods and Trader Joe's deal only with cage-free eggs, and Safeway is moving in that direction. Seeing large businesses make choices to avoid food tainted with animal misery encourages me to do the same. While cage-free does not mean misery-free, it is a step in the right direction.

*Eat free-range.* A decision to eat free-range pork and free-range, pasture-fed-only beef may mean that you will eat less meat. It costs the rancher more to wait four years for a steer to get big enough on pasture grass to take to market, so we would expect to pay more for the beef from such an animal. The same would be true of free-range pork, or free-range turkey or chicken. While I'm making this argument as a principle for eating just food to minimize animal misery, we also reap health benefits when we eat this way. Animals allowed to roam around and eat how and what their digestive systems were created to eat are healthier than animals fattened up quickly on unnatural diets laced with antibiotics to stave off disease and illness until they are big enough to take to the slaughterhouse.

*Be wary of the cage-free label.* The potential for loopholes and corruption has always plagued human intention to do good. For example, the labels "free-range" and "cage-free" have an inconsistent and troubling history. If you know your farmer, of course, you can know if your eggs are from chickens that roam around a barnyard. I'd been to Ed and Mary Etta's farm and watched the hens peck at grass and dust bathe. But I used to pay big bucks for eggs from "cage-free" and "free-range" chickens until I learned chickens can be crammed into pens instead of cages and technically still be labeled "cage-free," and that the eggs of a hen that has access to a barnyard through a little door at some point in her otherwise caged-up life can still be labeled "free-range," even if the hen never actually sets foot in the dirt. Pasture-fed beef could mean the steer was fed on pasture the first six to nine months of life before being sent off to the CAFO. But the truth is, all steers start on the pasture for the first six to nine months. Their digestive systems can't handle more than about six months of a corn-fed diet before they get too sick to slaughter for meat consumption. *Make the better error.* So no, we don't always get what we pay for. Unless we know the farmer or can see the operation, we can't fully trust the free-range, cage-free labels. The system can be abused, but I don't want to let that stop me from efforts to avoid animal misery with my food choices. We can err on one of two sides. We can try to shop ethically and sometimes get taken in by false advertising, or we can continue as we always have and justify it by assuming that the system is hopelessly corrupt and that nothing is *really* fair and just anyway. It seems to me that erring on the side of just food, even if it means I get duped from time to time by unscrupulous marketers, is the better error.

Green America offers an impressive array of information on all these issues, including being corporate watchdogs, holding companies accountable that claim they are doing good, and informing us of those that make little or no effort to be so (see chapter resources for more information). Green America assumes responsible shopping means using our power as consumers to be good citizens in our local and global communities. While being responsible shoppers also tends to be better for our own health and well-being, justice is the primary focus of the website. It shouldn't surprise us (but it seems to) that what is best for me and my family is often also what is best for the chickens whose eggs we eat, the cows whose milk we drink, and the pigs, cows, chicken and fish we eat.

People like Ben DeVries, founder of Not One Sparrow, a Christian voice for animals, encourage us to see a picture of the gospel stretching beyond caring for people to include redemption for all God's creatures. Our belief that God gave us animals to use as we see fit makes it challenging to turn the treatment of animals into an issue of justice. DeVries, a graduate of Trinity Evangelical Divinity School, is working to bring a fuller understanding of the gospel message of redemption, one that includes our care for animals.

## PRINCIPLE 4: EAT LOW ON THE FOOD CHAIN

It's not flattering to think of ourselves as part of a food chain, but we are. As omnivores, we can eat both meat and plants, and as smart omnivores we have figured out ways to sanitize our meat eating so we rarely think about the gruesomeness of it as it appears in nature, as illustrated for those of us who have outdoor cats.

An unclaimed cat in our rural Oregon neighborhood decided to take up residence with us; Mark and I obliged him. We call him Mrs. Pollifax, after a delightful elderly widow in Dorothy Gilman's novels who decides to become a spy for the CIA. Our cat shares only this in common with the character: both *seem* naively gentle and helpless, yet both are amazingly resourceful and able to be savagely savvy when they go hunting for criminals or field mice.

Mostly we call Mrs. P. "Pollifax" now that we know he's a he, rather than a she. We feed Pollifax well enough, but he continues to do what his cat nature inclines him to do—that is, catch, kill and eat, mostly mice but occasionally moles. He eats what he kills, which I prefer to the pattern of more domesticated cats that deposit creatures like trophies on the doorsteps of their homes. But he does offer us a tip of sorts on our welcome mat: the stomachs of mice, and the stomach, head and claws of moles. I imagine he leaves them in appreciation for the various services we render him, though Mark is more cynical than I am about Pollifax's ability to be appreciative.

I've watched him eat a mouse a few times because it fascinates me that he can eat around the stomach so tidily. He consumes the creature rather quickly—in less than three minutes. I won't go into detail, but it is rather amazing what cats do with their animal instinct.

We humans have distanced ourselves from the most vicious images of eating meat. I would be concerned if I found Mark eating a raw chicken on the patio, whether or not he ate tidily around the stomach. Except for a few fish caught on family vacations as a child, I've never killed anything I've eaten. Not until this year had I participated in the dressing process for a chicken I'd consumed, and I've never done so (or wanted to) for a cow, sheep, pig or deer. Our food-chain activities involve clipping coupons, making grocery lists, shopping for sales and preparing food that's already pretty much prepared. The farther removed we get from the growing and harvesting of plants, and the raising, slaughtering and dressing of animals, the more we lose touch with ethical questions surrounding responsible production and consumption of food.

**Eat your grain directly.** In the United States we make our way through 17,600 pounds of grain *per person per year* (Indians, by comparison, use about 4,400 pounds per person per year). That's forty-eight overwhelming pounds a day! Tending to eat high on the food chain, we consume almost all of that indirectly, meaning we get more of our calories directly from animals rather than from plants (Indians, who eat a lot of rice, consume more of their grain directly). According to the U.S. Department of Agriculture, Americans eat about 6.7 ounces of grain directly every day, and most of that is refined (white bread, Captain Crunch cereal, white rice) rather than whole grain (whole wheat flour, oatmeal, brown rice). The bulk of the grain we consume is hidden in our food, like the corn syrup in our soda pop, or fed to the cows and chickens we eat. We eat better, live healthier and demand less from the earth when we consume the bulk of our grains directly, rather than indirectly, and as whole grains, rather than refined ones.

According to calculations made by Earth Policy Institute, a Washington, D.C.–based research organization, if everyone ate the diet of an average U.S. citizen, the earth could feed 2.5 billion people well. Italians use about half the grain we do, and if everyone ate like Italians, the earth could sustain 5 billion people well. If we all ate the way they do in India, the world could feed 10 billion people well. Our current world population is 6.8 billion. Assuming everyone gets on board with limiting family size and with a lot of global cooperation, we could possibly level out the world's population at 8 billion by 2040. Once those numbers sink in you realize that a compassionate table will hold a lot more bulgur, rice, beans and lentils than meat.

The image of eating at a compassionate table is wonderfully inviting, but figuring out *how* to eat compassionately is a bit more difficult. It involves being mindful of the people I share this planet with, and probably eating somewhat differently than others do in my neck of the global woods.

*Intentionally move down the food chain.* A complicating variable to the population growth is that as income levels rise in countries around the world, people tend to move *up* the food chain. Earth has handled the increase in population okay, but for the first time in history, in addition to the population explosion of the last hundred years, more people are eating more animals that have eaten plants, rather than eating the plants themselves.

Learning how to eat lower on the food chain can be daunting. But good help is available from older food cultures, and from folks among us who have always eaten lower on the food chain. During my first year of nursing school a new cookbook hit the press. Doris Janzen Longacre compiled the *More-with-Less Cookbook* in 1976, and Marla, one of my suitemates, gave me a copy. Now, thirty-some years later, we handle the tattered and splattered pages of the spiral-bound paperback gingerly. Longacre compiled the book in response to what came to be known as a world food crisis, when food shortages—especially throughout Europe—got the world's attention in the late 1970s. Readers were encouraged and shown how to integrate more brown rice, barley, lentils, nuts, and local fruits and vegetables into filling and delicious meals. The *More-with-Less Cookbook* has been printed fifty times and has sold nearly a million copies. Longacre just thought she was helping other Mennonites think about eating less so others could eat enough; she had no idea the book would sell so broadly. Her book is one of many that helps us learn to think about food differently, and to eat in ways that are healthful for ourselves and mindful of those for whom food availability is not a given.

Vegans eat lowest on the food chain with their plant-based diets. They have a reputation for being somewhat obnoxious. Sarah, my sweet-tempered, hippy-like, vegan daughter, has, in the past, criticized her own tribe for being compassionate eaters when it comes to animals, and somewhat less compassionate when it comes to animal-eating humans. Sarah is one of the nicest, kindest vegans I know, and one of the most committed. She sports a henna-colored tattoo on the inside of her wrist that simply reads "vegan."

When Sarah comes home she fills it with new fragrances and tastes. We've created Indian feasts complete with homemade naan, and rolled out ravioli from scratch and filled it with a pumpkin and hazelnut filling. One Christmas she gave me a recipe box filled with handwritten recipes. She inspires me to eat low on the food chain by making it easy.

Vegans and vegetarians are intentional about food choices often for a combination of reasons: to avoid participating in an industry that mistreats and abuses animals, because it's healthier, to consume fewer of earth's resources so that others might have enough, and because it is the most sustainable way to eat. Mark and I eat low on the food chain for all four reasons; we didn't set out denying ourselves certain foods for the sake of denial. We savor homemade multigrain molasses bread (mostly on Sunday nights—it's a sabbath rest sort of thing to make bread on Sundays) and fruit cobblers from berries and peaches we froze from the prior summer's bounty. We make stews and soups in winter, and spinach, asparagus, corn and bean salads in the summer. We love food. Every meal we honor God's creation and give thanks for its abundant variety. We love the endlessly creative ways you can combine beans, wheat, rice, oats, lentils, seeds, nuts, corn and an assortment of vegetables and fruits. Some of our meals take fifteen minutes to toss together; most of them take between thirty and forty-five minutes. On occasion, like when I work with Sarah, we cook and bake for an afternoon—a gift to others and a pleasure to ourselves.

I do not intend this as an argument against eating meat. Some of my best friends eat meat! Eating meat can be done with intentionality and justice. When our daughter Rae and son-in-law Aubry got married, they wanted to feed their guests local, pasture-fed, free-range chickens. So Rae hunted around for a farmer in Yamhill County who could raise thirty-five chickens for a wedding in July. We held a picnic dinner after the wedding, where people brought sides and salads, and we provided bread from a local bakery, barbecued chickens from Kookoolan Farm, barbecued portabella mushrooms for the nonmeat eaters, and sun tea, lavender lemonade and wine. We celebrated their marriage with good food, with just food. And it tasted grand. The goal is not to become vegetarian or vegan, but to become intentional about how we eat. Eating wisely, courageously and with moderation allows us to fully celebrate and enjoy good, just food.

**Combine both of the above and eat a low carbon diet.** In 2007 Bon Appétit Management Company implemented the Low Carbon Diet. How and what we eat contributes to climate change; a low carbon diet makes the connection explicit. This decision was perhaps the most challenging test of Bon Appétit's commitment to being a socially responsible company, as some consumers would be decidedly unhappy with how it affected them.

Foods that contribute to a high carbon diet include the meat and cheese we eat; anything air-freighted and needing refrigeration such as fresh fish, or fruits and vegetables grown elsewhere and fragile enough to need either air freighting or refrigeration in the transportation process; our food waste; foods that have been highly processed and then shipped hither and yon; and foods with various forms of disposable packaging. Some of this will be unpacked more in the chapter addressing climate change. For now, note that when we eat whole foods (oatmeal, for example, involves minimal processing and packaging; Cheerios has eleven ingredients that are gathered, processed and packaged), local food, seasonal food and low on the food chain we are eating a low carbon diet that is good for us, good for our neighbors and good for our planet.

Denny Lawrence, the Bon Appétit director at George Fox University, gave employees and students a heads-up explaining why he planned to implement changes in support of the Low Carbon Diet. To lessen our university's carbon footprint, the cafeteria decreased the beef it served by 25 percent, tropical fruits (bananas, pineapple, mangos) by 50 percent and packaging by 10 percent.

Some folks missed the beef and bananas, and Denny heard a fair bit of grumbling from some who felt they weren't getting what they were paying for, but Denny said most of the feedback was positive. Generally people want to make choices that help the world be a better place. Belonging to an organization that takes a stand for justice strengthens our sense of identity as a community in action. I like belonging to a community where students not only hear talk about justice, courage, wisdom and moderation but also see us seeking to live out the virtues we call forth in our students.

## A FINAL WORD

When you sit down to a spinach and beet salad from your farmers' market, to chicken that comes from a local farmer, and to coffee that has been grown in sustainable ways that do not harm the earth and was bought for a fair price, you are eating *abundantly.* Nutrients nourish your body and contribute to the well-being of others, making connections with near and distant kin that move us toward greater hope for *shalom*—peace because justice prevails. Through just food we assert our citizenship in the world.

I summarize the principles with a few queries to help you think practically with an eye toward virtues regarding how you feed your-

self and your family. For the record, my family doesn't eat virtu-
ously or justly all the time. We've only recently weaned ourselves
off of non-fair-trade chocolate chips. The impetus to leap from paying $1.79 for a twelve-ounce bag of chocolate chips at Fred Meyer to
paying $8.95 a pound for them from Sweet Earth Organic Choco-
lates came through the writing of this chapter. It rubbed at my conscious that we, a high chocolate-chip-consuming family, still bought
non-fair-trade chocolate chips, even though we've been buying fair-
trade cocoa for some time. I hadn't known how bad the industry
was until I looked into it and learned that with its use of child slavery to work in the fields, it is one of the most human-rights-abusing
industries. I am yet some distance from where I want to be in just
eating, but I'm farther along than if I'd never begun, and taking one
step at a time to get there. Here's to beginnings.

- *Am I eating in ways that treat people who grow my food with
  dignity?*

- *Do the people who grow and harvest my food have enough to eat
  themselves and to provide for their family's basic needs?*

- *Am I eating in ways that support and celebrate my local community?*

- *Am I eating in ways that treat the animals that provide me with
  food humanely and with respect?*

- *Am I willing to go without something so that I can afford to pay
  farmers what it costs to raise animals respectfully and without
  human-induced suffering?*

- *Am I eating in ways that are sustainable for future generations and
  that benefit rather than harm (or do limited harm to) soil, water,
  bugs, birds, bees and the air?*

- *What decision can I make today (this month, this year) to eat more
  just food?*

The *More-with-Less Cookbook* inspired a nation of budding

cooks, moving us collectively from ideals to real food choices. For most of us, what food we eat feels like a personal choice affecting only our family and the people we invite into our homes. Yet we have a responsibility and power to look beyond our homes and make the world more just. As we recognize God's goodness and sustaining power, we can also recognize a call to participate as God's representatives and steward-gardeners in creation.

Sitting at tables of compassion involves asking hard questions about how I can eat more justly, but it is also about joy, laughter and sharing God's goodness in community with others. Food, celebration, building and bonding relationships—all of these contribute to the well-being of our body and the well-being of others with whom we live in the world. But this can all feel overwhelming too. Food preparation and gardening happen to be activities I like, and in general things we like are things we're good at. You don't all have to become bread-baking, pesto-making, home-grown hospitality junkies to eat just food or to celebrate the goodness of food. All you need to become more intentional about what you eat is to learn something about where your food comes from. Start with one of the queries and challenge one choice at a time. Maybe you'll start buying fair-trade coffee, or find a place to get cage-free eggs, or track down your nearest farmers' market. Start somewhere and see what comes of it.

o    o    o

## RESOURCES

*How can I find farmers' markets and Community Supported Agriculture (CSA) in my area?*

- Local Harvest. This site doesn't list them all, but it will get you started. You can also check your local newspaper, city hall or city/county information.

*220 21st Ave.*

*Santa Cruz, CA 95062*

*www.localharvest.org*

- USDA Agricultural Marketing Service tracks farmers' markets. The following link assists people in finding farmers' markets in their area: http://apps.ams.usda.gov/FarmersMarkets.

- Natural Resources Defense Council. An environmental action group combining the grass-roots power of 1.2 million members and online activists.

*40 West 20th Street*

*New York, NY 10011*

*Phone: (212) 727-2700*

*www.nrdc.org/health/foodmiles/*

- Local Community Supported Agriculture (CSA): www.nal.usda .gov/afsic/pubs/csa/csa.shtml

- FoodRoute. A national non-profit organization dedicated to re-introducing Americans to their food. The link below offers general information on eating locally and getting involved in local food efforts.

*37 East Durham St.*

*Philadelphia, PA 19119*

*www.foodroutes.org*

**How can I learn more about a low carbon diet?**

- Bon Appétit supports a full website with information.

*100 Hamilton Avenue, Suite 400*

*Palo Alto, CA 94301*

*www.circleofresponsibility.com*

- http://bonappetit.typepad.com

- www.eatlowcarbon.org

- www.circleofresponsibility.com/page/321/low-carbon-diet.htm

### Where can I go for recipes for locally grown and in-season foods?

- Lind, Mary Beth, and Cathleen Hockman-Wert. *Simply in Season* (also commissioned by the Mennonite Central Committee to promote the understanding of how the food choices we make affect our lives and the lives of those who produce the food). Scottdale, Penn.: Herald Press, 2005.

- Longacre, Doris Janzen. *More-with-Less Cookbook* (commissioned by the Mennonite Central Committee, a relief, community development and peace organization of the Mennonite and Brethren in Christ churches). Scottdale, Penn.: Herald Press, 1976.

- Madison Area Community Supported Agriculture Coalition. *From Asparagus to Zucchini: A Guide to Cooking Farm-Fresh Seasonal Produce.* Madison, Wis.: Jones Books, 2004.

- Mennonite Central Committee—World Community Cookbooks. This is essentially all of the information on everything. www.worldcommunitycookbook.org/links.html

- World Community Cookbook. A guide to in-season fruits and vegetables—how to prepare and use them. www.worldcommunitycookbook.org/season/guide/index.html

### Where can I find fair-trade chocolate and coffee?

- Divine Chocolate. This is a farmer-owned (as in African farmers) company. Their webpage is definitely worth checking out even if you aren't in the market for chocolate.
  *418 7th Street SE*
  *Washington, D.C. 20003*
  *Phone: (202) 332-8913*
  *www.divinechocolate.com (for store)*
  *www.divinechocolateusa.com/about/ (for story)*

- Sweet Earth Organic Chocolates. They offer chocolate chips, baking chips and shavings, as well as specialty chocolate (like chocolate Easter eggs).

  *1491 Monterey St.*

  *San Luis Obispo, CA 93401*

  *Phone: (805) 544-7759*

  *www.sweetearthchocolates.com*

- Dean's Beans. They have baking cocoa, great chocolate espresso beans and coffee.

  *50 R.W. Moore Ave.*

  *Orange, MA 01364*

  *Phone: (800) 325-3008*

  *www.deansbeans.com*

*How can I learn about raising chickens in my urban backyard, and whether or not I'm allowed to do so? While we're talking about chickens, where can I learn more about the treatment of chickens in egg factory farms?*

- Urban Chickens: www.urbanchickens.org

- The Humane Society of the United States: www.hsus.org/farm/resources/animals/chickens/

*How can I learn more about the Millennial Development Goals (MDGs) and the Micah Challenge?*

- For a list of the goals, current actions and updates on progress see the United Nations official site: www.un.org/millenniumgoals/.

- Micah Challenge USA is the U.S. branch of an international Christian organization committed to helping eradicate global poverty: www.micahchallenge.us/

*Where can I find out about a company's trade and labor practices?*

- Green America is a not-for-profit membership organization whose mission is to "harness economic power—the strength of consumers, investors, businesses, and the marketplace—to create a socially just and environmentally sustainable society."

*1612 K Street NW, Suite 600*

*Washington, D.C. 20006*

*Phone: (800) 584-7336*

*www.coopamerica.org/programs/responsibleshopper/*

- Global Exchange is working to build people-to-people ties in the global economy, fighting on behalf of fair trade for workers worldwide.

*2017 Mission Street, 2nd Floor*

*San Francisco, CA 94110*

*Phone: (415) 255-7296*

*www.globalexchange.org/campaigns/fairtrade/*

# PRELUDE

## The Teeth and Tongue

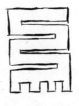

*Ese ne keterEma*

During my freshman year of college I found myself walking through a small, rural market in Thailand. Hundreds of textures, smells and noises engaged my senses. Plastic bags full of orange-colored boba tea, produce, live chickens, Western hand-me-down clothes, toys, computer parts, wristwatches and art lined the streets.

In the center of the market I came across a small girl who couldn't have been more than four or five. She sat on her knees, in a bowed position, with a small bowl in front of her, a position of begging. As I knelt down and looked into her face, the liveliness and excitement of all the new sights, sounds and smells faded. I became fixated on one thing: how I could possibly help her. I dropped some Thai baht into her bowl and continued on my way through the market, her image lingering. Purchasing some food, I retraced my steps to take it to her, and then continued on my way again. But thoughts of her still demanded my attention, so I returned again with some small yellow and red sandals to go on her bare feet.

I left the market feeling helpless. I wanted to help this girl, to *really* help her in a significant way—not just put food in her belly for a day or two or give her shoes that she would grow out of soon enough—but I didn't know how. I was overwhelmed by her abundant need in the face of my abundant wealth and paralyzed by the fact that I didn't know how to transfer one to the other. I've continued to think about her through the years, and pray that she didn't end up like many poor rural Thai girls, being tricked or sold into the sex trade. Her large brown eyes, timid smile and quiet "thank you" are forever etched into my mind.

I wish, however, that I thought of her every time I went to a market or grocery store in the United States, or used my purchasing power on the global eMarket. If I thought of her it would keep me honest and consistent: consistent between the values I preach and the values my choices reflect. It would remind me that I want to value the well-being of children like her above the *things* that fill my life. It would also remind me that many of my buying choices impact boys and girls around the world. One of the effects of living in an interconnected and interdependent world is that the coffee, cocoa, skirts, telephones and shoes I buy are connected to children, women and men everywhere. Often the connection is distant and indirect, to people who, for example, live in a small rural town in Malawi that used to use its land for subsistence farmers but now uses the majority of its land for cash crops for Westerners. Tea and tobacco are two big ones in Malawi. Sometimes the link is more direct. Perhaps my purchases are connected to a young woman who sat at a sewing machine for hours without bathroom breaks, being paid unjust wages as she made my dress. Or maybe my purchase is linked in a positive way. The Christmas gifts I purchased for friends and family from Ten Thousand Villages benefit women and men who are being paid fairly for the beautiful crafts they make.

In the reality of interdependence and connectedness the inevitable question ought to be, when I buy something, am I contributing to the well-being or to the harm of others, including young children like the one I met in the Thai market place? I stopped to see and acknowledge the face of the young Thai girl; I'm not always so gracious. I have passed by many hungry and cold women and men on the streets of Chicago, Portland and New York without taking time to look into their faces.

Emmanuel Levinas, a Lithuanian-French philosopher and Jewish Holocaust survivor, talks about the significance of the face-to-face encounter. Upon seeing the face of the other, he claims, one must do everything possible to meet the other's needs. It's a radical theory, and a nearly impossible way to live. I've noticed that when I'm not prepared to meet someone's need, whether it be someone asking for money or someone wanting to cut in line, I don't look at him or her. Looking someone in their eyes, seeing their humanity and denying their need is unbearable, particularly when we are in a position to help them.

Seeing the faces behind what we use and purchase is the starting point for refusing to be complicit in the suffering of others through our consumption patterns. But this takes effort; the way global transactions work inevitably keeps these faces invisible. It takes a lot of work to search out and then choose to look into the faces of the invisible. It does not happen overnight. I have often gotten ahead of myself, thinking I was an enlightened compassionate consumer only to realize it was more complicated than I had yet realized!

During my second year at Princeton Seminary I became a vegan. With that decision I thought I'd finally figured it all out. I had already made progress avoiding sweatshop labor, trying to buy the majority of items secondhand and purchasing fair-trade gifts whenever possible. I was excited to finally dine at a compassionate table too. While I was still in my über-zealous vegangelical stage my roommates and I held a poetry night. I made vegan chocolate chip cookies to serve up with our poetry readings. After a friend ate one and proclaimed how great it was I excitedly pronounced that they were vegan, "completely compassionate chocolate chip cookies." In the middle of pronouncing the "completely compassionate" bit I stopped in my tracks, realizing this was not completely honest. The chocolate chips were not fair trade, so while animals were treated justly, cocoa farmers were not. My so-called compassionate vegan cookies ended up being less compassionate than I thought. I had made the animals' faces visible but had failed to look for the invisible faces of children who had been trafficked or sent to labor on cocoa farms. Maybe I had the animal thing right, but I realized I still had a lot of learning to do when it came to dining compassionately. For years I'd thought about how other people were connected to my clothes and my coffee, and how animals were connected to my diet, but I hadn't delved into the complexity of how my food choices impacted other humans.

It's moments like that one that make me realize becoming a compassionate consumer will be a lifelong journey, and I'm okay with that. It's exciting to know there is always potential for growth and renewal. The global market is so integrated and complex that it takes constant attention and awareness to avoid being complicit in the suffering of others.

The Akan symbol *Ese ne keterEma,* translated "the teeth and tongue," is associated with the Akan proverb *"Wonnwo ba ne se,"* translated "no child is born with its teeth." We improve and advance. Just as our bodies mature and grow, so it is with our souls. As we grow in our compassion, love and mercy, we grow to be more like Christ.

Children can't even sit up on their own until about six or seven months. Growth and development is slow and gradual. We give babies plenty of time, grace and cheering as they explore and develop new and exciting motor skills. We can give ourselves the same grace as we journey in sharpening and developing our capacity to be compassionate consumers.

Often I am impatient with myself; I want holiness, sanctification and compassion that is microwavable. But the really important things in life take time, patience, persistence and energy. Being a compassionate person is one of those really important things in life.

Seeing faces is a powerful starting point—choosing to do the work to look for and at the faces behind the products we purchase. For me it means transporting the image of the little girl I met in the Thai marketplace to the marketplaces I frequent in the United States or, more likely, the global online marketplaces I frequent. But this is a hard transition. It means shifting the way I think about my economic decisions, reorienting and adjusting variables like being "trendy" or saving money. Growing my consumer values to be compassionate and life-giving to others is a constant challenge. At times I knowingly look away, or simply let myself stay comfortably unaware. But *I* have seen their faces.

I need to remind myself of that when I go to the marketplace so that I might reveal the light of Christ *even* through my shopping, or perhaps *especially* through my shopping. The way we emulate Christ in the marketplace is a lifelong journey full of growing pains (like giving up Hershey's chocolate that entices me from the check-out stand) and joyous growth that comes from the satisfaction of contributing to the well-being of other people and communities through my purchases.

---------------( 4 )---------------

# LIVING IN
# THE MARKETPLACE

*Ruin in its worst form is inevitable if our national life brings us nothing
better than swollen fortunes for the few and the triumph in both
politics and business of a sordid and selfish materialism.*

—TEDDY ROOSEVELT, 1910

Here's a partial list of nonfood things that I purchased in the
two weeks before writing this chapter: rain chains (from eBay) to
replace some of our downspouts (an unnecessary but attractive
change to our house), a gift for my niece and her new baby daughter, two valences for my windows at work, three lavender plants,
four mochas and five pairs of socks.

Even if Roosevelt correctly predicted an inevitable ruin emerging from selfish materialism, buying mochas, rain chains and
books is good for the economy. In addition to voting and work
(either volunteer or paid), taking care of your children and staying
out of trouble, being a good citizen includes consuming things.
When successful advertising agencies get us to buy stuff that didn't
exist a decade ago (think bottled water in coin-operated machines—positioned beside the drinking fountain no less!), they

are not only making money for their stockholders, they are also strengthening our country's economy. That we buy cases of bottled water when water that meets higher standards runs free out of our faucets ought to make us shake our heads in befuddlement, wondering how the marketers did it. But whatever else we say about it, buying even bottled water is good for the economy.

Consumerism, that is, our preoccupation with and inclination toward buying things, is a relatively young phenomenon in the history of civilization. Not until the industrial revolution did we have a mass-production system that made affordable products for the masses. The move of chickens from family farms to factory farms that we witnessed in the last century followed a similar move that had happened in the garment industry, the auto industry and furniture making the century before. Mass production meant lower prices. No longer was consumption primarily a pastime for the upper class; now it came to define the middle class, who also had access to affordable clothing, dishes, cars and appliances.

A hundred years after Roosevelt's prediction we have become identified by what we purchase—our brand and style of clothes, cars, house and hobbies. And while Roosevelt referred to a selfish materialism ruining the fabric of society, runaway consumerism also bumps into conversations about walking gently.

So as a product of the twentieth century I'm torn between two goods: that of frugality and simplicity, and that of being a good citizen as defined by responsible consuming and enjoyment of the ingenuity of new products. The frugality side means I chide myself for not borrowing stuff, or buying used, or listening to the voice that tells me I am about to be snookered by advertisers if I buy what I'm standing in the aisle contemplating. The responsible consumer side encourages me to let go of my guilt, to spend money responsibly, and to let myself enjoy sitting on the porch and watching and listening to the rain as it cascades down the rain chain.

You likely identify with that tension. So besides food choices, how do we think carefully about the decisions we make regarding clothes, household furnishings, remodeling and refurbishing projects, hobbies, and vacations? The bulk of this chapter unpacks seven principles that help us make ethical choices. We are going to buy stuff; whatever tension we feel is useful when it motivates us to use our purchasing power to support ethical sectors of the economy. And companies that promote justice and good stewardship of earth's resources are out there. So before we get to the principles, I want to highlight some good news.

## CONSUMER POWER AND CHANGING MARKETS
Whether or not the invisible hand of the market works in quite the way Adam Smith supposed it would, consumers help shape how companies do business. Smaller companies have an easier time choosing to be ethical. They can find a niche, stay small and do the world a bit of good by exchanging money and products in sustainable ways that support local communities here and abroad. None of the companies listed on Green America's National Green Pages, a listing of socially responsible companies, are large ones. You wouldn't recognize most of them. Once a company goes big, the pressure to use shortcuts to make them more competitive is hard to avoid. The ones that seek to be socially responsible anyway are worth supporting. They are trusting that their customer base is strong enough to keep them afloat.

A number of groups rank corporations every year, coming up with lists of the best and worst on an assortment of variables. Among Fortune 500's list of the winners for the largest, highest-revenue-producing companies are Exxon Mobil and Walmart, who have traded places for first and second place for the last few years. Neither of them rank high for social responsibility. In contrast, Starbucks, Google.com, FedEx and UPS are examples of big companies that consistently rank high on social responsibility lists. I'll highlight just one of them.

In 2004 Starbucks joined the UN Global Compact, a voluntary international network of corporations and organizations that support ten principles related to justice for people and environmental sustainability. One of Starbucks's goals is to purchase all of their coffee from fair-trade or direct-trade sources by 2015. In 2007 Starbucks launched Cocoa Practices, a pilot program with buying guidelines for obtaining cocoa grown in environmentally sustainable ways and purchased so that farmers, laborers and the local communities are respectfully and fairly treated. Thirty percent of Starbucks cocoa was purchased under Cocoa Practices in 2008, and Starbucks's goal for 2009 was 35 percent. Transparency is part of what makes a company accountable. I found the Starbucks report online, and anyone with Internet access can do the same. Some companies make this available; many do not. I couldn't find a comparable report for either Walmart or Exxon Mobile.

Smaller, more innovative companies are making a difference in the world too, and they also get noted. Green America has its own People's Choice Award for a green business. In 2008 Mountain Rose Herbs, a small company that employs sixty people out of Eugene, Oregon, won the award. Mountain Rose Herbs is committed to clean transportation (all of the company vehicles use locally produced biodiesel), fair trade, becoming a zero-waste company (last year the company produced less waste than a typical household of four) and producing 100 percent organic products. Success is possible so long as it is not measured by profits.

As the public becomes more aware of unethical practices *and begins to demand change,* responsive larger companies will move toward greater transparency, accountability and social responsibility. Choosing to support socially responsible companies with our purchases is one part of walking gently in the marketplace. But there is far more we can do. Following are seven principles that can guide you as you attempt to walk gently in the marketplace, focusing choices on ethics and goodwill. My goal is to par-

ticipate in the marketplace responsibly, appreciatively and compassionately. Sometimes that involves welcoming ingenuous
products into my life; always it involves resisting the compulsion
to buy now, buy lots, buy blindly and strive to have it all.

## PRINCIPLES ONE: GIVE FIRST

I know, I know, you've heard this since your early days in church
when your mother gave you a dime to put in the collection plate as
it went by. Once I realized that God didn't actually get the money
(I had wondered what God did with it anyway), I thought ministers preached about giving and passed collection plates around to
be sure they'd get their next paycheck. Some of them do, but I've
come to understand that it takes money to free the church to minister to its congregation, community and the world. Besides, giving money away keeps us from thinking we are entitled to every
dollar that comes our way.

Over the decades Mark and I have honored our early training to
give. We have supported our local church, along with other endeavors to make the world a better place. Both Mark's parents and
mine valued hard work and responsible living, and gave us reason
to believe that working hard would be rewarded with a middle-
class lifestyle. It helped that they were in a position of some privilege (that is, they were white; lived in towns with well-functioning
schools and in a homeland that was not experiencing civil war,
drought or famine; and were not addicted to alcohol, drugs or
gambling). We all control some aspects of our economic destinies,
but a chunk of it is determined by our heritage. Tithing can remind us that our middle-class life isn't simply a reward for being
responsible. It's also about being born at a particular time and
place, into a particular ethnicity and social class.

When you give some of what you have away it helps remind you
that you are not entitled to it. John Wesley, the eighteenth-century
theologian and Anglican cleric, encouraged Christians to work

hard, live frugally and give away all they could. He lived what he preached, never living on more than the twenty-eight pounds he first earned as a young man and giving the rest away, primarily to the poor, even as his family grew. Contemporary Christians such as Shane Claiborne and Ron Sider are modeling the same kind of radical giving—graduated tithing—where the more you make, the more you give away, primarily in ways that bring justice to the poor.

Most of us won't take vows of poverty and live like Shane Claiborne. Mark and I still have a retirement account, have invested in a home, spend more than we can believe on our hobbies (currently bees, chickens, gardens and our apple orchard), and have a cushion of savings on which to draw if the furnace goes out or if a family member needs some financial help. Yet we want our faith to shape our choices at least as much as the recommendations and requirements of our current economic system. Investing in retirement, for instance, makes sense given that our families tend to be nuclear and autonomous, rather than extended and interdependent. Yet adopting Christian values of charity, equity and justice may require rejecting, or significantly modifying, marketplace wisdom that encourages personal accumulation of wealth through spending, investing and saving.

A first principle for walking gently in the marketplace is to give generously. It reminds us that we are not entitled to what we have, and to both hold it loosely and discover the joy of living more simply, and giving more away.

## PRINCIPLE TWO: LIVE WITH MARGIN

The economic troubles accompanying the first decade of the twenty-first century remind us that living well in the marketplace includes living with fiscal responsibility. As a nation, we spent the last half of the twentieth century learning the joys of buy now–pay later credit. We've stood as witnesses to the devastating ways that debt can catch up to us, most particularly in the mortgage crisis that resulted in over six million foreclosures by the beginning of 2010, with more predicted to come.

Financial guru Dave Ramsey talks about avoiding credit debt altogether if you can. Use a credit card, but pay off the balance every month. If you can't pay off the balance, stop using it. Work toward paying off all debt—car, school, even your house. And save. Start with a one-thousand-dollar emergency fund first, and build up savings worth three to six months of your expenses. Build margin. The less debt you have, the more freedom you have to give, to take time off work to pursue other interests, to exhange a high-paying, unsatisfying job for a lower-paying, more satisfying one.

A silver lining in the economic woes of the last few years is that we are all relearning to live within our means, rather than above them. Americans are leaning into this task out of necessity. Regaining financial balance and margin allows us to live well in the marketplace, rather than frantically trying to hold together a life unraveling madly at the edges.

## PRINCIPLE THREE: SHARE AND BORROW STUFF
Mark and I are not good at this principle. But we try. I made a recent attempt and borrowed my mother-in-law's pressure cooker to can green beans. But then she ended up borrowing someone *else's* to can her own beets a day or two later. While Donna was very gracious about borrowing someone else's canner because I had hers, I have since purchased my own. Rather than borrow a chipper we bought one. How often will we use a chipper? We do live on a forest that sheds big branches in storms, we reasoned, and who wants to loan out their chipper anyway? We have a toolshed full of tools for every occasion. We could open a rental store, or a tool library. I've heard of churches and communities that have such "libraries." Starting one is not so farfetched for us, actually, because we loan our things out more easily than we borrow them. I need to pay attention to my own principle here, but I imagine a lot of people are like me.

When we share our stuff through borrowing and loaning we walk more lightly because fewer hand tillers, pressure cookers or lawn mowers need to be manufactured. That's a statement of the obvious, but a lot of us have been convinced we need to own everything we use. When we borrow and loan we also strengthen our community ties. We learn the blessing of interdependence, of giving and receiving, and we craft memories and strengthen friendships as we share our things and the stories that go with them.

We have some friends who live in an intentional community. They have lived out this principle well. The four families borrow Steve and Dianne's pick-up truck when someone needs one. Gregg and Elaine put up the backyard pool, and another family maintains the backyard jungle gym. They are preserving the "do you have a cup of sugar?" sort of drop-in neighborliness that doesn't much exist anymore. So they come and go into each other's homes and lives, sharing their stuff and their time, and creating an interdependent community.

I don't mean to idealize their situation. Sometimes they miss their lack of privacy, and sometimes communication gets muffled, along with feelings. But they are raising their children in a community that shares and is open to each other's needs and joys. They borrow, loan, give and take to and from each other, modeling what's possible when we engage the marketplace as small communities rather than individuals.

### PRINCIPLE FOUR: REUSE, BUY USED, RECYCLE

In *The Contented Soul* I tell a story of a chair I rescued from the dump. One of the neighborhood norms in Wheaton, Illinois, was for people to put household goods out on the curb that someone else might find valuable. They did so a day or two before garbage pick-up. People could cart off whatever treasures they found; unclaimed goods went into the garbage truck and ultimately the landfill. Suburban dumpster diving without the dumpster.

That's how I found the chair that now graces my office. Beneath white cracking paint oak emerged, weather-worn but beautiful. I reglued some lose connections and wrapped the yellow plastic seat with upholstery fabric covered with leather-bound books in rich hues. To say I "redeemed" the chair might be a bit sacrilegious. But maybe it's a perfect illustration, taking something that has lost value and beauty and reclaiming, refinishing and repairing it. Since God does that with us, is it possible God also delights to redeem a creation that groans for redemption?

North Americans have developed an art for exchanging used goods with each other. From garage and yard sales to Craigslist, informal community events and networks prove that we don't have to get all our stuff boxed, plastic-wrapped and tagged from a store to be happy with it. Churches and civic clubs use rummage sales to raise money, and neighborhoods use block sales to help out with spring cleaning and to get neighbors talking after winter's seclusion as they exchange names (sometimes for the first time) and greetings along with lamps, wine glasses and children's toys.

We walk gently whenever we buy used and recycle our things so they can be used yet again. As I said, we have a chipper, but we bought it for forty bucks from a friend's garage sale. Mark gave me a snazzy wooden gizmo that allows me to dry out the plastic bags I reuse until they get holes in them. Mostly he meant it as a joke, but he washes out bags and hangs them upside down to air out too. Most towns have secondhand stores, or Goodwill stores, where canning jars, pots and pans, clothes, party favors, decorations, and small appliances await redemption.

A general rule of thumb for walking gently is to avoid one-use-only products. So I have To-Go-Ware, a fork, spoon and knife (and chopsticks!) that I keep in the car and pull out whenever I need silverware, and try to remember to take a container for leftovers to restaurants. I used to take my own glass to faculty lunch since our university used disposable plastic glasses for that event. (I'd like to think we now use washable glasses because I kept nudging the Bon Appétit director, Denny Lawrence, about it, but I also know he is committed to sustainability and always looking for ways to improve our food practices.) We use cloth napkins at home, and have added to our supply over the years so we can use them when we have larger gatherings over. We bought an extra set of inexpensive silverware and plates some years ago to use if the gathering is large, and if I don't have enough glasses, we pull out our pint-size canning jars. Yes, it requires more cleanup, but that's a price we're willing to pay to offer our guests real cutlery (no plastic fork breakage or paper plate drips!) and to keep garbage out of landfills.

Buy a travel coffee mug for coffee you purchase at the espresso drive-through (the secondhand stores will have scads of them), and take your own ceramic mug to coffee shops. Have you ever noticed how much better coffee tastes out of ceramic rather than paper with a plastic lid or, goodness gracious, out of *Styrofoam*? Besides, increasingly coffee shops are giving discounts to people who bring in their own mug as a way to encourage good citizenry.

Get a water bottle (I use aluminum given the controversies around plastic) and fill it with your free tap water to avoid purchasing one-time-use water bottles. Take your own bags shopping. When you buy one-use items, use paper plates and cups rather than plastic ones, and when you buy paper products, use those made from recycled and postconsumer paper. Finally, when you use one-use products, recycle them so that the resources that went into creating them in the first place can be used again.

More could be said, but I'll leave it at that. Get creative.

## PRINCIPLE FIVE: PURSUE JUSTICE FOR PEOPLE USING YOUR CONSUMER POWER

When Mark and I decided to purchase only fair-trade chocolate bars, chocolate chips and cocoa, I expected that to mean we'd eat fewer chocolate chip cookies since fair-trade chocolate chips are expensive. Mark thinks it ought to mean we eat *more* of them, not less. Why not be extravagant, he asked, and buy a lot of fair-trade products that benefit the communities from which they come? Once he understood some of what happens in the cocoa industry—such as child trafficking, as well as the economic desperation that drives some parents to sell some of their children into bonded labor so they can feed their other children—he didn't want to buy M&M's or Toll House chocolate chips anymore. So why not buy lots of fair-trade chocolate chips to reward the companies that promote human justice and allow farmers in other countries to make a reasonable wage? Mark just ordered ten pounds of them! For the record, at this point we still drink mochas and hot chocolate when we go out. We are still complicit, but less so, and year by year are untangling our complicity and using our consumer power to work toward justice in the area of chocolate and cocoa.

We can use our consumer power to pursue justice by rethinking our gift giving as well. Ten Thousand Villages, a non-profit fair-trade program run by the Mennonite Central Committee (MCC), started global fair trade sixty years ago. The MCC runs stores in eighty-one cities and an online business besides. A broad array of all-occasion gifts and items for your own use can also be purchased from SERRV, another non-profit fair-trade online business, and Global Exchange. See the resource section for links to their stores as well as their history, vision and mission. Granted, you won't find fair-trade MP3 players, barbecue grills or basketballs, but starting with the assumption that you want to use your consumer power to pursue justice for people opens a door of unique ways to think about gifts.

Figuring out how to buy just clothes begins a complex conversation. For example, the garment industry is the backbone of Cambodia's economy, providing jobs for 270,000 women (mostly) that then provide a livelihood for 1.5 million Cambodians. So when Gap or Banana Republic sets up a garment factory, they are providing better-paying jobs than what is available otherwise. Moreover, since a sweatshop job is a better option than prostitution, some economists say buying clothes made in sweatshops is good global citizenry. However, other economists (and many sociologists) squirm at that, tracing a history that includes colonization and exploitation of countries that now provide the cheap labor for multinational corporations (MNCs). Once tribes and villages gathered and farmed informally, providing adequately for their families and communities, but colonization took away their sovereignty, their right to continue farming as they had for generations. Fields that villagers used to grow or gather food was leased or sold to MNCs by the dictators in charge of their governments, and over time factory work became the only employment available that paid enough to buy rice to feed their families.

This controversy between the good of providing jobs that are better than no jobs or prostitution, and the bad of perpetuating an exploitive form of dependency the West created in the first place, has not been resolved, and it is more complex than my short summary suggests. Given the existence of the Global South garment industry and other sweatshop-like industries, the International Labour Organization (ILO), an arm of the United Nations, fights to hold MNCs accountable to provide safer, more humane working conditions and to pay employees a livable wage.

Those who want to buy clothes without supporting questionable labor practices have several options. The most basic one is to avoid giving money to companies whose practices are questionable. People can buy clothes from resale or Goodwill shops, supporting resale enterprises, or they can buy clothes made in the United States, Canada or Europe. Some fair-trade apparel is available, but if you are looking for jeans, slacks or those cute little black evening dresses, you probably won't find them.

Holding steady against pressure to replace our wardrobes every couple of years is also a way we can stand against both consumerism and questionable labor practices. By refusing to succumb to fashion gurus who tell us we *have* to stay in style to be relevant, attractive and successful, we support walking gently in the broadest sense. Styles change just for that purpose—to keep us purchasing clothes we don't need. I wish I had the courage to wear one or two outfits to work every week. But I feel students and colleagues mustn't see me wear the same outfit even twice in two weeks. What kind of *crazy* thinking is that?! What if a community of coworkers, especially women, stood together on this? Imagine what the lot of us could accomplish if we refused to buy clothes made by women and children unless they were paid a livable wage and constructed under working conditions we'd find acceptable for ourselves and our children?

I can summarize the various points made about consumer power with the broadly criticized Walmart corporation, the world's largest private employer with over two million employees. On the upside Walmart brings low-cost products to small towns and rural communities that can't attract other superstore chains. Groceries, clothes, household products, electronics and automotive goods available in the suburbs come to rural communities through Walmart at prices the lower-middle class can afford. But the high cost for those low-cost products is becoming increasingly unacceptable to communities, boycotters and social activists. In short, Walmart is criticized for being bad for local businesses (who can't compete and are pushed out of business), bad for communities, which tend to become *poorer* after Walmart moves in (money that once stayed in the community, boosting the local economy through local businesses, now goes back to the Walmart corporation and stockholders), bad for employees (for multiple reasons—one is that they can't afford the health-care benefits offered), bad for women and children working in sweatshops around the world, and bad for the environment (Walmart repeatedly breaks environmental law).

Walmart was started by a Christian family, and the primary benefactors of the Walmart business are now extraordinarily rich family members. That bit of information adds to the sensitivity of talking about the company, making it particularly uncomfortable for Christians who want to believe Christian businesses do more good than harm in the world.

Walmart is under pressure to become more accountable for their policies and to put people (all people) before profit. One way to do that is to join the groundswell of folks pursuing justice by fighting on behalf of communities trying to keep Walmart out, and on behalf of employees and foreign workers associated with Walmart. A second way that any of us can work toward justice is to speak with our dollars, to shop where the shopping promotes justice and well-being for local and global communities.

## PRINCIPLE SIX: DO NO HARM— PROTECT ECOLOGICAL SYSTEMS

Minimizing harm to ecological systems may be more realistic than doing *no* harm, but by aiming high maybe we'll protect against our tendency to set our goal too low. As we've said before, human well-being cannot be separated from the well-being of the rest of the ecosystems. What's good for animals, fish and birds, water and air, forests and soil is also good for us.

You can start by freeing your own house from cleaning supplies using toxic synthetic chemicals. Switch to green cleaning detergents; the biodegradable, phosphate-free label is a good start. Some adventurous folks make their own cleaning supplies. Baking soda, vinegar, ammonia and rubbing alcohol will clean just about anything. Mixing the ingredients and putting them in a spray bottle doesn't take much time. Changing our cleaning supplies is more a matter of changing our habits than making an investment in time or money. We get used to buying Tide laundry detergent, become loyal customers and forget that other products could do the work more gently. Yes, we *can* get our clothes, dishes, sinks, windows, floors and toilets clean using natural, even ordinary ingredients. I doubted this for years, sure that the products on the grocery shelf had to be superior. Sometimes they are; after all, toxic chemicals are toxic for a reason.

It is not particularly comforting that talking about household cleaning products and toxins, reminds me of cosmetics, but it does, maybe because we think about safety and health in both cases. The FDA does not require animal testing for cosmetics, yet many companies continue to test on animals anyway, partly because the labs and jobs are already in place and partly because these companies believe U.S. consumers want to be sure their mascara will not make them go blind or kill their child if she or he ingests it. This was another industry I preferred to ignore. I mean, how bad could it be, really? I didn't have to look very deep to decide I didn't want to consume in a way that suggests my right to mascara that won't irritate my eyes is more important than the well-being of rabbits whose eyes are injected with the stuff day after day to see how much suffering and eye disease it causes (I'm toning this down here). There is also the Lethal Dose (LD) test, where animals are tube fed, injected with or made to inhale the toxins in cosmetics to see how high a dose is required to kill some predetermined percentage of them. Animals die from convulsions, bleeding through the eyes, nose, mouth and anus, vomiting . . . need I say more? Is there some other way to be sure I won't go blind from using my mascara?

Fortunately yes. Otherwise the European Union may not have voted to ban animal testing from all cosmetics. But those of us living in the United States have options too. If you use cosmetics you can purchase ones that have not been tested on animals. Hundreds of companies, including Avon, Mary Kay and The Body Shop, do not use animal testing to ensure the safety of their products. Other tests offer more predictable results anyway. Some companies avoid the problem altogether by using only nontoxic substances in their cosmetics. What a brilliant idea.

From cleaning supplies to cosmetics to carpets, we can make choices to minimize harm to ourselves, animals and ecological systems. We can purchase carpets manufactured in sustainable ways that will not end up in a landfill in eight to ten years, and lumber that has been harvested responsibly and sustainably. In some cases you will pay more for sustainably manufactured or harvested goods. You can look at it as having to pay more because producing carpets and lumber in responsible and sustainable ways is more costly, and recognize that you are absorbing more of the true costs that come from consuming products from earth's resources. We allow earth's various ecosystems to flourish when we use sustainable ways to draw out the resources we use.

But like I said, what we've already known for some time, and this ought to be a big selling point, is that what is good for the animals is good for the people eating the animals. The Great Lakes became a key place of concern over thirty years ago, as multiple industries used it as a dumping ground for toxic waste. Fish living (and mostly dying) in the Great Lakes were contending with DDT, pollution from leaded gasoline, and PCB (polychlorinated biphenyls—a chemical compound used in transformers and coolants). All of these have been banned in the United States, and the Environmental Protection Agency (EPA) has been actively working to restore the site and reduce pollution. As a result health is improving for eagles, falcons and osprey, for fish, flora and fauna, and for people who draw on the Great Lakes for sustenance.

Again, lessening our harm to earth fosters our own health. Cancers have been linked to the toxins that became everyday in our lives through the petroleum-based products that made their way into the plastic we wrap, cook and store our food in, through the VOCs (volatile organic chemicals) in our carpets and paints, and through the pesticides and herbicides we use on plants.

Because the Do No Harm principle is most clearly linked to our own well-being, you'd think it would be the most compelling one. But it isn't, partly because products that may harm us are ingrained in our lives—taken-for-granted pieces that we cannot imagine *really* harm us. Isn't that what the FDA exists to do? To rat out harmful practices and substances from our lifestyles? We believe that if something was really bad for us the government would do something about it before we were harmed overly much. Unfortunately or fortunately, depending on your perspective, the marketplace is driven more by corporations than our government, which, after all, is elected in part by the big bucks of corporations supporting particular officials.

Prosilac offers an example of the difficulty in getting the FDA to ban a drug already banned in Canada and many countries in the European Union. Prosilac is a growth hormone (referred to as rGBH) used to increase milk production in cows. Monsanto, a powerful pharmaceutical company, produced it. After extensive studies on rGBH, researchers concluded that it is definitely bad for the cow, and most likely bad for the consumer. But turning research findings into policy to get Prosilac taken out of production in the United States has been a tangled mess. The negative press may have been what propelled Monsanto to sell the rights to Prosilac to Eli Lilly in 2008, a company with global rights to produce Prosilac and convince farmers in Africa, Latin America and Southeast Asia that they need it for their dairy business. Regardless of the FDA's support for Prosilac, some U.S. grocery chains (such as Kroger) and businesses (such as Starbucks) refuse to buy rGBH-containing milk.

It is overwhelming to try to pursue the Do No Harm principle in all directions, so pick one for this year. Learn how you can use your power as a consumer to minimize or do no harm and make the change. The resource list includes a few potential starting places. Besides being good for us, we become more *humane*, more compassionate stewards and caretakers of God's creation when we do what brings health to other creatures.

### PRINCIPLE SEVEN: SEEK CONTENTMENT

Walking gently also comes from wanting less, from finding joy and contentment in what you have already, or from what is abundant and free right in front of you. Mark and I enjoy evening walks, and can spend an hour on a summer evening sitting on lawn chairs watching our chickens scratch in new areas looking for bugs, dust bathe, chase after flies and butterflies, and clamor for the aging beans, corn and strawberries we toss their way. We find that recreational, though realize most wouldn't. Some kind of free recreation is available to all of us. Most large cities and many small towns offer free outdoor concerts, movies in the park, and other ways of enjoying our communities and friends without having to spend money. Berries are often abundant for the picking along roadsides in the country (though I wouldn't always recommend picking them!). The invitation of naps on the sofa, reading on the porch, making music—all these are free and simple gifts.

That's one reason we celebrate the fall equinox and the winter solstice. We want to be reminded of the gifts of seasons that allow for the flourishing of spring and summer. That life slows down in the winter is a universal goodness—giving earth a rest, and us all time to slow down our active lives and reevaluate where we are spending our time, energy and money. In winter Mark and I plan for spring planting, read up on what we don't know, take classes in beekeeping and anticipate a new season with new possibilities.

Contentment includes slowing down and taking note of the simple and beautiful that exists all around us. Earth has seasons and cycles, and rejuvenates and replenishes all on its own because God is there—sustaining it and inviting us to praise, worship, and enjoy the beauty and abundance all around.

## CONCLUSION

Marketplaces in the Global South are colorful, aromatic, bustling places where vendors sell chickens, fish, vegetables, grains and fruit, freshly baked chapatis, cloth, bags, and shoes. Bounty, skill and labor come together in the marketplace. Individuals support each other and their communities as they exchange money for goods, or in some cases, goods for goods. When you know the neighbor who is selling you eggs, and are counting on your neighbor to buy your shoes, there is a built-in accountability to be neighborly.

If we could see the mother selling eggs as her daughter sits nearby reading a book, or the man squatting by the fire baking chapatis, or the child peddling a big bunch of bananas—perhaps especially if we knew their names—we would desire justice for them. Perhaps if cosmetic testing labs had glass walls we would even want justice for animals.

We engage the marketplace whenever we walk down the aisles of stores, but also when we give money away, or choose to make our own nontoxic cleaning products, or buy used instead of new. There are numerous ways we can walk gently as we buy the stuff we need and want. Find a new one, one you haven't tried before, and . . . see what happens.

o   o   o

## RESOURCES

*How can I learn more about issues related to consumerism and products and companies that do harm?*

- Watch the documentary *The Corporation* (prod. Mark Achbar, dir. Mark Achbar and Jennifer Abbott, 145 min., Big Picture Media Corporation, 2004), winner of the Sundance Film Festival for best documentary. See <www.thecorporation.com/index.cfm> for more information, as well as updates on corporate activity.

- Check out the National Green Pages on the Green America website: www.greenamericatoday.org/pubs/greenpages.

- Chocolate Company Scorecard offers a critique of major chocolate companies and how they rank regarding issues of justice. The critique is conducted by the International Labor Rights Forum.

  *2001 S. Street NW, Suite 420*
  *Washington, DC 20009*
  *202-347-4100*
  *www.laborrights.org/files/ChocolateScorecard09.pdf*

**Where can I go to learn about sweatshops and sweatshop reforms?**

- ILO (International Labour Organization) is a United Nations agency that brings together governments, employers and workers to promote decent work throughout the world. This is an excellent international resource.

  *4 route des Morillons, CH-1211*
  *Genève 22, Switzerland*
  *www.ilo.org*

- Watch the documentary *Shop 'Til You Drop: The Crisis of Consumerism* (prod. and dir. Gene Brockhoff, 52 min., Media Education Foundation, 2010). The film can be previewed online at www.mediaed.org.

- Ethical Corporation was founded in 2001 and is an independent company that helps businesses work toward corporate social responsibility.

  *www.ethicalcorp.com/*

**How can I learn more about Christians choosing radical lifestyles?**

- For starters read Shane Claiborne's *The Irresistible Revolution: Living as an Ordinary Radical* (Grand Rapids: Zondervan, 2006).

*What fair-trade organizations have products for purchase online?*

- Ten Thousand Villages, a non-profit store run by the Mennonite Central Committee, provides fair income and dignity by providing a market for artisans in the Global South.
  *www.tenthousandvillages.com/php/about.us/about.vision.php*

- SERRV International works to eradicate poverty worldwide through fair trade. www.agreatergift.org/

- Global Exchange builds people-to-people ties, works to curtain sweatshops and addresses environmental issues.
  *www.globalexchange.org*

*Where can I find sweatshop-free clothes?*

- For some great background information on this topic go to <www .greenamericatoday.org/pubs/realgreen/articles/nosweatshops.cfm>.

- For union-made apparel from the United States and Canada see <www.nosweatapparel.com/>, <www.AmericanApparel.net> or <www.justiceclothing.com>.

*Help me get started using earth-friendly home products.*

- Here's my mother-in-law's recipe for window washing solution: to a quart jar add 2 cups isopropyl alcohol, ½ cup ammonia and 1 teaspoon liquid dishwashing soap. Fill up with water and transfer to a spray bottle. Another simple solution: use borax instead of caustic cleaners in your toilets, tubs and sinks.

- See <www.eartheasy.com/live_nontoxic_solutions.htm> for more ideas.

- For a list of companies that use recycled paper for tissue, napkins and paper towels, go to the Natural Resources Defense Council's link at <www.nrdc.org/land/forests/gtissue.asp>.

*Where can I find out which cosmetic companies don't use animal testing?*

- www.leapingbunny.org/indexcus.php

- www.idausa.org/facts/costesting.html (In Defense of Animals website)

**What are some other alternative gift-giving ideas?**

- Join with others and give a portion of a pig, sheep, chickens or a cow for a family in the Global South using an organization like Heifer International.

  *1 World Avenue*
  *Little Rock, AR 72202*
  *www.heifer.org*

- Make gifts—bake bread or cookies, make soaps or books—or give gifts of your time, such as planning a shared activity or adventure, rather than giving things.

- Buy gifts from any of the fair-trade organizations listed above.

# PRELUDE

## God Is in the Heavens

*Nyame Bíríbí Wo Soro*

During my junior year at Wheaton College while walking toward Blanchard Hall I came across a thin brown leather wallet lying on the ground. Picking it up I discovered it wasn't a wallet at all but a paper gospel tract that *looked* like a wallet. The wallet opened into a pamphlet that began with the following question: "If this had been a real wallet would you have taken the money? You probably would have (or else why would you have picked up the wallet)? Therefore you are a sinner" (simplified version). From there it went on to discuss the Romans Road and to articulate how a sinner such as myself could be reconciled with God.

While I commend the creators of this tract for their creativity, I was bothered by the message. I wondered what I found so unsettling and irksome about it since I agreed with the major thrust of the theology. It occurred to me that what bothered me was that it started with the bad news, with trying to convince me I was a bad person.

The tract is like an advertisement designed to convince you something is missing from your life (brighter teeth, smoother skin, a healthy colon, more stylish clothes) that makes you inadequate. If the advertiser succeeds you'll feel worse about yourself. To remedy that situation you will hopefully buy their product to become like the smiling, beautiful, social people in their commercials. Advertising is a tactic built on our fears of inadequacy. The tract followed a similar model, attempting to convince me I was lacking something and then "selling" me their solution. By listening to the news, or opening myself to the many cries of desperation in the world, I know that something is dramatically awry in the world; I didn't need convincing of that. The world is in need of a savior. *I* am in need of a savior. I let these theological thoughts linger.

*Nyame Biribi Wo Soro* means, "God is in the heavens" or "something is in the heavens." It is a symbol of hope and inspiration. It is associated with the proverb *"Nyame biribi wo soro na ma embeka mesna,"* which translated means, "God there is something in the heavens, let it reach me." This symbol of hope reminds us that God's dwelling place is in heaven where God listens to our prayers as Creator and Redeemer. It is to the heavens we look for a hope, a dream or inspiration to keep us moving through hard times and to imagine a better world.

A few years after I picked up that tract, I found myself in the midst of an engaging conversation in seminary. We discussed how, up until the last five hundred years, theology began with the doctrine of creation as the starting point, but since the Reformation much Protestant theology has used the Fall as its starting point. Yes, yes, we start with the creation story, but we quickly jump to the Fall and move on from there, as though the Fall is the significant part at which God's plan comes into play. "Isn't it odd," I chimed in, "that since the Reformation, presenting the gospel has mostly meant convincing people there is a problem? So we start with bad news rather than the goodness of creation."

The Hebrew worldview in the Old Testament included the belief that the savior and redeemer of Israel was also the creator of heaven and earth. In other words, Israel's savior was their creator, which meant the purpose of the savior had to align with that of the creator so the rich patterns of right relationships would extend to all creation, bringing harmony and satisfaction among all creatures. This was shalom.

Because the redeemer was also the creator, restoration involved the whole earth, likely the whole cosmos. A full hope for the future encompassed all of creation: the wolf and the lamb lay together, the calf and the lion, the infant and the cobra all live in peace (Isaiah 11:6-8).

When our theology focuses more on God's plan to deal with the Fall than on God's hope for creation, we can't help but view God primarily as Redeemer rather than first and foremost as Creator. Creation becomes the backdrop for redemption, no longer valued and seen for its own goodness and reflection of God's character but primarily functioning as the means of our redemption. With the Fall as the starting point, the focus centers on solving our sin problem and theology is built around this core issue. The focus is on *our* sin, *our* separation from God. We more easily overlook the goodness of creation and the restoration of the whole cosmos.

But Jesus is the Word incarnate, the Word that was with God from the beginning. God created everything through the Word, which gave life to everything that was created (John 1:1-4). The Creator is our Redeemer, the earth's Redeemer.

I'm not suggesting we aren't sinful or that we aren't in need of a redeemer. We desperately are. But the danger of a Fall-based approach is that the goals of redemption are narrowed down to reconciling our individual souls with God. The fullness, wonder and magnificence of the good news get lost. Besides, this focus on reconciling our individual souls to God makes it difficult to know how to fit that redemption plan into disappearing ice caps or the koalas losing their habitat. We need and have a Redeemer who created earth; sustains the seasons (Genesis 8:22; Job 38:32); cares for the land and visits, waters and enriches it (Psalm 65:9-13); and provides grass to the desolate wasteland (Job 38:26-27). The Creator-Redeemer takes care of the animals, providing them with food (Psalm 147:9; Job 38:41); unties the ropes of the wild donkey, liberating him and providing him with the wasteland and salt flats for his home (Job 39:5-6). Our Creator-Redeemer watches when the mountain goats and the does give birth (Job 39:1-2), mourns with and addresses the land, and limits the impact of human warfare upon it (Jeremiah 22:29; Deuteronomy 20:19-20).

When we understand that the Redeemer's goals align with that of the Creator, caring for earth is part of the gospel message of redemption. Romans 8:19 discusses how creation eagerly awaits for the sons and daughters of God; the redeemed sons and daughters of God help to liberate creation from its bondage. This is why conversations about climate change, how we consume energy and natural resources, and our environmental responsibility are not periphery conversations to be had but are essential to the larger conversation about redemption and the kingdom of God. This is a matter of redemption.

"God there is something in the heavens, let it reach me." The "something" in the heavens is the One who empowers us to imagine a better world. The One who came to redeem us and the cosmos is the same One who created the heavens and earth, the eternal Word. God's creative Spirit empowers us to imagine a better world, and the hope and dream of a better world inspire our redemptive work.

God has honored humanity by empowering us to be part of the process of God's redemptive plan. This is a hopeful and empowering message. When I picked up that paper wallet I did not feel empowered or hopeful; I felt shamed and burdened. The plans of the Creator are much bigger, and much more exciting than that.

# 5

# A MATTER
# OF DEGREES

*What mighty praise, O God,*

*belongs to you in Zion.*

*We will fulfill our vows to you. . . .*

*You take care of the earth and water it,*

*making it rich and fertile.*

*The river of God has plenty of water;*

*it provides a bountiful harvest of grain,*

*for you have ordered it so.*

—PSALM 65:1, 9

I avoided Harry Potter through all the years that J. K. Rowling wrote about him. Shortly after the final book made its debut, Sarah told me I should read the seven-volume tale. "Really, Mom, you'll like them," she said. "I'll bring you the first two when we come visit for Thanksgiving." So I started the first one over Thanksgiving break and stayed captivated enough to finish the last of Rowling's 4,160-page story before classes resumed in January. ("Oh to be reading Harry Potter for the first time!" my friend Elaine said as she loaned me books four through seven.)

For the few of you who have not read them, Rowling tells a contemporary tale of wizards, witches and muggles (ordinary, non-magically endowed folks). While the story on the surface is about Harry Potter and his friends learning to make potions, weave spells, ride broomsticks and use wands at school, the darker story line is one of a bad wizard who lost power but is gaining it back, and wants to control the world. There comes a point (around book three) that the evil wizard has risen again. The wizardly world has two responses. The first, adopted by the legal arm of the wizardry world, is not to believe it. The Ministry of Magic thinks announcing the news would cast unnecessary fear into people and require a rather drastic change of focus, altering life as they were comfortably living it. They wanted more definitive evidence before acting.

The second response was to believe what no one wanted to believe and to begin to strategize how to combat the wizard before he regained his full strength and compiled so large an army that any action would be too little, too late.

I don't imagine for a moment that Rowling intended this to be a metaphor for global climate change, yet it works well enough and was on my mind as I read. If one wanted to build an argument for erring on the side of caution when it comes to climate change, Rowling does that rather effectively.

Are we in a global climate change crisis or not? And if so, does human activity make a significant contribution to it?

We can find experts on both sides of the argument, and I wanted to know whom to trust. Like a lot of folks, I'm wary of being swayed just because I'm swayable. We tend to trust science well enough—science brings cures for cancer and depression, better communication technologies, cleaner energy and safer cars. Yet a lot of us, like the wizardly world in Rowling's novels, tend to be more skeptical of scientific reports that require something of us. For the last 150 years Westerners have tended to trust the progress brought by new ideas and technology. But when we cannot see a direct and personal benefit of accepting some idea that requires something of us (perhaps giving up our incandescent light bulbs), we sometimes respond with fear and bludgeon it to death before we examine whether or not the idea is dangerous or helpful. We embrace science that brings us progress we like; we are more skeptical of science that would take us on uncertain paths that might cost us comfort, convenience or money. This conversation leads down one of those paths. So let me say up front that deciding to respond to global climate change does *not* require a total reversal of our way of life. Some of the most significant changes we can make are rather small.

Richard Kerr, an oceanographer and senior writer for *Science* magazine, reported in April 2007 that an international community of scientists (several hundred) had concluded that the global warming debate was settled. For the first time they also felt confident asserting that humans had a significant influence over it. Getting that many scientists to draft a document they could all sign was no easy task. The group of scientists from all six continents analyzed and synthesized relevant literature and studies as part of the United Nations' IPCC (Intergovernmental Panel on Climate Change). It's a report that landed the committee the Nobel Peace Prize in 2007 for their effort to understand climate change, educate the world about what they discovered and jumpstart the thinking about how to counteract it.

Still, not everyone agrees with the report. Not even all the climatologists, physicists and geologists agree. Many, like Christopher Field, an ecologist from Stanford and a coordinating lead author on the report, say the findings are reported far too conservatively. In February of 2009 Field addressed the American Science conference in Chicago and said data on greenhouse gas emissions from 2000 to 2007 show the severity of global warming over the next century to be much worse than the IPCC report estimated. Warming feedback loops have led to faster warming than earlier models predicted. International grass-roots movements like 350.org emerged to coordinate global efforts to communicate to world leaders a need for an aggressive commitment to reduce carbon emissions. Ordinary people planned over 5200 events in 181 different countries that all took place on October 24, 2009, to let leaders gathering in Copenhagen that December to hash out climate change policy know the people around the world were invested in the outcome. Others, like Harrison Schmitt, an Apollo 17 astronaut and past senator from New Mexico, are skeptics, and believe the global warming we are seeing is part of earth's natural warming and cooling cycles. We haven't caused whatever warming we're seeing, and neither could we possibly stop it. It is a force of nature—not a product of humanity.

I, like most of you, wanted to know who to trust. After all, 2008 was the coolest year since 2000; might that suggest all this warming up is just a natural cycle of warming and cooling?

To find out what scientists were saying about climate change, off and on the record, I decided to attend one of their meetings. The American Scientific Affiliation (ASA) annually gathers scientists who are Christians to hear about each other's research, share ideas and talk the talk. The bulk of presentations in the 2008 meeting had something to do with climate change.

My primary conversation partners ended up being physical science engineers. Two were particularly helpful in shedding light on who lines up where in the global warming conversation. Most of my conversation with Jack, who has taught engineering and worked in industry, took place during a birding expedition. Over our sack lunches eaten at picnic tables during one of our stops, Jack claimed that the mainstream scientific community (about 96 percent of them, he said with engineering precision) believed humans to be significant contributors to global warming. He claimed his number came from articles in both *Science* and *Nature*—two publications of the scientific community. I asked him about the other 4 percent, and he thought that some skeptics worked in industry, and so had an interest in understating human culpability in climate change. Some people's politics made it difficult for them to give the evidence a fair read, as they couldn't set aside their assumption that global warming was part of a liberal antigrowth agenda. Others were not mainstream scientists but politically conservative folks with charisma and a platform (for example, novelists, journalists, people in business, maybe astronauts) who have read a lot, but don't know the scientific language and don't have the skills to interpret the data themselves, or to validate or invalidate others' interpretations of the data. Jack said skeptics could be, and often were, a combination of any of the above.

However, I didn't have to look hard to find Tom, a physical engineer in chemical technology development, who came from the skeptics' side. I ate lunch in the cafeteria with him the next day. He is among those less swayed by what he considers "the politics of global warming." There may or may not be a crisis, but humans certainly don't have the power to cause one if there is. When I asked him why the majority of his colleagues in science think there is a crisis and that humans have contributed significantly to it, he said he believes (along with other global warming skeptics) that scientists teaching and researching in university settings have succumbed to pressure to be on a particular side of this issue for the sake of career advancement, or to get grants, because it is currently the only acceptable opinion. It is politically unpopular and unacceptable, Tom said, to be a skeptic of human-induced climate change. I wondered if evangelical Christian scientists would be more likely to be in the 96 percent or 4 percent crowd, and how much faith and politics affect how scientists read data.

My limited conversations reinforced what I've been reading and observing: those working for chemical and petroleum companies tend to see this issue differently than those working in the academy.

Oriana Zill de Granados found something similar. She is a production director for the Center for Investigative Reporting, and has served as a senior producer of *Hot Politics* for Frontline. Granados investigated the backgrounds of five top skeptical scientists of global warming and found them all to have financial ties to oil, auto, electric and coal industries. This seems to be rather significant information. But then, I'm an academic and thus already predisposed to trust other academics—the larger group of climatologists, meteorologists, geologists and biologists who say we are in a global warming crisis and that human activity is a primary contributor to it.

At this point in the climate-change conversation most scientific scholars agree that human activity has contributed significantly to the climate change we are experiencing. We are already in the crisis, they say; it is not something that *will* happen if we don't change our behavior soon. They outline the devastating effects climate change is having and will increasingly have on people, animals, insects and plant life, especially those living in coastal areas, islands, deserts and the Arctic and Antarctic regions. Most also focus on what we need to do to decrease the level of carbon dioxide in the atmosphere, bringing it back down to 350 parts per million (ppm) in our atmosphere from the current level of 390 ppm. The conversation is complex and multifaceted. But it does not have to be overwhelming.

## JOINING THE CONVERSATION
We are God's representatives on earth, and fulfilling our role as stewards might require us to join the conversation and take a deeper look at what scientists in industry and professors of science are saying about climate change. Walking gently for me was first motivated by praise and awe for God who created and sustains the earth, but eventually I came to recognize that humans have particular vows to fulfill that include being stewards of God's creation.

For me, joining the conversation meant learning what scientists who share my faith were saying about climate change. Keith Miller, a geologist at Kansas State University, introduced ASA conference attendees to earth's history as understood by geologists. He talked about cycles of climate change, and the feedback loops that bring about an ice age or a global greenhouse. I didn't know, for instance, that earth's orbit varies, and that earth oscillates or wobbles as it journeys through space around the sun. These variations take a long time, and explain warming and cooling as inevitable parts of earth's long-term history, and future.

Miller did say that as we burn coal, oil and natural gas we are artificially returning (or oxidizing) carbon that has been stored since the last ice age, raising the level of carbon in the atmosphere and warming things up. Still, I couldn't tell how strongly Miller believed human activity contributed to the current climate change.

Wanting clarity, I emailed him after the conference and asked (as respectfully as email allows) if I could surmise from his presentation that humans aren't the *only* or *primary* cause of climate change. Did he believe global warming was a natural occurrence, with humans speeding it up a bit? Miller quickly apologized for his lack of clarity. He wrote:

> The current release of greenhouse gases by the burning of fossil fuels is without question a major contributor to the current increases in global average temperatures. What is unique about the climate change now occurring is not the magnitude of change (from a long-term geologic perspective) but that it is being significantly caused by us. Such increases in global temperature and $CO_2$ levels have not occurred for over 400,000 years. Human populations, particularly the poor and those already living at the margins economically or environmentally, will be significantly affected.

If humans are *not* causing this global warming, then perhaps our best conclusion is that God is ushering in a new era, however unpleasant (or unlivable) for the current creatures living here. Maybe the "Earth's Next Chapter" perspective helps those of us who rather love earth's current beauty and diversity to remember heaven is our home, not earth; we're just a passin' through.

But I don't find that satisfying anymore, or theologically sound.

I grew up believing that heaven and eternity matter, not earth. Later, though, I learned that it wasn't until after the Reformation that the Fall became the centerpiece of a theology that placed more emphasis on heaven to come than on the broken world we inhabit now. Pre-Reformation theology was rooted in the goodness of creation, and African and Eastern Christians, Catholics, and Anglicans still reflect that theology. They remind us that God created, called it good and loves the entire cosmos. Earth cries out for redemption, and God's long reach into the future included redeeming earth from before the beginning. We've been called to participate in the work.

Maybe we can't slow global warming down enough to prevent the species, human life and land losses caused by increasing flooding and drought. But maybe we can. A lot of folks are assuming so and working to develop energy alternatives, and to change policies, minds and wills to get the rest of us to see what's possible. As a steward of creation and representative of God I want to live in a way that offers the greatest chance for life on earth to continue to flourish. I'm not supposed to give up; I shouldn't be the one to say, "Oh well, there's nothing I can do about it," as I rev up my Hummer. How would God have me—and you—live at such a time as this? What conversations will we start or join in our churches, places of employment and communities?

Understanding the conversation was a good beginning place for me. I wanted to know why global warming is controversial, the implications of global warming and what's being done about it. Following is a primer of sorts. Skim this section if it's more than you want to know right now. It offers enough of the backstory to help you think through the issues as you consider actions you might take and lifestyle choices—which is the focus of the next chapter.

## GLOBAL WARMING 101

In 1850 scientists began using thermometers to keep a record of earth's temperatures. Since 1880 the earth has warmed 1.4 degrees, and most of that—one degree of it—has occurred since 1970. In the Nobel Prize–winning report, the IPCC reported that eleven of the last twelve years were among the warmest since 1850. A rise of one degree has been enough to melt 25 percent of the Arctic ice cap, and to alert us that earth's climate is becoming unstable.

### What's turning up the heat?

Scientists don't disagree about whether or not the earth is getting warmer; what they disagree about is whether or not *humans*, a rather puny force when set against the power of the *whole* planet, could actually warm it up a few degrees. Think of a colony of ants trying to warm up five acres of forest. Probably not gonna happen. Earth has moved from glacial periods, where things were really cold, to interglacial periods, like we're in now and have been for the last eleven thousand years or so. That means those of us inhabiting the Northern Hemisphere can frolic in skimpy sundresses and shorts in the summer, and grow watermelon and tomatoes in our gardens.

The climate-change skeptics say that heating and cooling trends have to do with our planet's orbit and axis changes, not people. These shifts occur over thousands of years from weather patterns that create feedback loops, reinforcing cycles that freeze or heat up this dear, dear chunk of rock, soil and water loping through space. Right now the perfect combination exists and earth is chock-full of life.

Granted, that's an oversimplified explanation, and the earth scientists among you will cringe. It's probably also a bit troubling for those who believe the earth is less than ten thousand years old. I always had a hard time figuring out where the dinosaurs and ice ages fit into the history of the Bible. Eventually I decided it made sense that God introduced Adam and Eve during this most recent interglacial period when earth was good and ready to foster the flourishing of human, animal and plant life as we know it. That's a bit oversimplified too, but I'll let it stand, as it leads to a different conversation.

However God fit in the dinosaurs and ice ages, the point is that earth has been through cooling and heating cycles before. But as near as the climatologists and geologists can tell, a difference between one of those cycles and the warming trend we are currently experiencing is that previous trends took place over several centuries; this one is occurring in less than one hundred years.

*How* puny humans (in the big scope of things we really are quite small) are raising earth's temperature is a reasonable question. The academic world explains it roughly this way: The sun's rays burst through our atmosphere bringing light and warmth to our planet. Most of the heat bounces off; ice caps are particularly good at reflecting heat back into space, which is a good thing or we'd be cooked. Think of the colors we wear in summer and winter. The fashion rule of white after Easter and black after Labor Day wasn't merely fashionable. Light colors in the summer keep us cooler by reflecting the heat of the sun. Similarly, dark colors in the winter absorb the heat of the sun and offer extra warmth. The right amount of warmth is captured by our atmosphere and absorbed by the ocean and land, keeping us adequately warm at night and not too hot during the day, fostering life on earth.

Mostly the atmosphere is made up of nitrogen and oxygen. It is the increase in gases called "greenhouse gases," such as carbon dioxide, methane and nitrous oxide, that raises concern. These gases, which are important to our well-being in the right concentrations, are particularly good at absorbing the sun's heat and keeping the planet warm. We've always had some of these gases in the atmosphere, but as the concentration of them rises, so does earth's temperature.

**Where do these extra greenhouse gases come from?**
Greenhouse gases come from living life. They come from simply breathing, from warming and cooling our homes, from traveling. Greenhouse gases are released when we till the ground for our gardens and crops, build homes and schools, print books and newspapers, raise cows and pigs. We also release carbon dioxide into the atmosphere any time we burn oil, coal and natural gas. Water vapor, the largest greenhouse gas and the one most capable of affecting weather patterns, is emitted through industry that sends plumes of vapor into the air as a byproduct of manufacturing, but also naturally—like when volcanoes erupt. Pollution (chemicals, biological materials, particles) comes from burning fossil fuel in our trucks, homes, schools, churches, hospitals and factories. We send a fair bit of that up in the air too, though the Global North pollutes the air less than we used to, which is a bit of good news in an overall not-so-good news story. Earth's atmosphere is a mighty big space. For the last eleven thousand years or so it has kept us just warm enough, holding in enough heat to keep us comfortable and letting the rest seep back into space.

Forests help keep the whole thing in balance. Trees absorb, or "capture," carbon dioxide and release oxygen—good, beneficial activities. Besides that, trees provide shade for other plants and wind and storm barriers that prevent landslides and flash floods. Trees also offer homes for an assortment of creatures, including humans, although we usually cut them down before we live in them, unlike the rest of the animal kingdom—except, I suppose, for beavers. Plants, especially trees, help keep the climate and the

carbon dioxide/oxygen gases in balance, the air clean, and earth's
creatures healthy. About the time we started measuring earth's
temperature we also started finding a lot more uses for all those
trees. In addition, the land underneath forests became prime real
estate ready for development, and the trees blocked progress. One
of our best balancing agents got significantly compromised. The
fact is, earth once had a heck of a lot more trees.

The particular thermostat bump noted that's occurred since the
1970s happened about the time oil production in the United States
peaked. As countries in the south industrialize, their use of coal,
oil and other resources increases too. China now uses more oil
than the United States, which was, until recently, the top consumer of oil, and significant greenhouse gas emissions come from
the coal burned in India and China to produce electricity.

But driving our cars and heating our homes do not primarily
cause global warming. Farming and food transportation practices
top the list, which is why we are hearing more about low carbon
diets these days. A 2007 United Nations study concluded that agriculture accounts for 30 percent of greenhouse gases. Twelve percent of that comes from tilling, fertilizing and transporting food,
and the rest comes from raising and "processing" cows, pigs,
chickens and other animals. By way of comparison, trucks, cars
and other transportation account for 13 percent of greenhouse gas
emissions. Isn't it interesting to learn that how we eat impacts
global warming more than what we drive?

A lot of people in my generation grew up eating a relatively low
carbon diet. Growing up in the 1960s in Arizona I never ate fresh
pineapple, although I do remember canned pineapple showing up
in pineapple upside-down cake now and again. I had never heard
of papaya, and Mom didn't have access to couscous, tofu, spring-
roll sheets or fresh fish flown in from the Atlantic Ocean. All of
those are available to me now. It takes a lot of fuel to get those
foods to the shelves of my oversized local Safeway.

Besides the carbon emissions from transportation of food, all those cows that used to be part of the family farm are now being raised in CAFOs. The poop at those local cow-raising operations gets dumped into special "lagoons" that then send high concentrations of methane and nitrous oxide gas into the atmosphere, and leak nitrogen-rich, sludgy stuff into local water sources. The locals aren't rejoicing over the abundance of manure in their neighborhoods. Yes, in small amounts nitrogen-rich cattle manure is a good thing. But too much of a good thing really is too much.

Our diets changed and so did our driving habits. Together they contribute a chunk to global climate change. We celebrated the end of the gas shortages in the 1970s by driving ourselves ever more hither and yon for our jobs, entertainment, shopping, errands and church. We traveled from suburb to suburb, or suburb to city, and back again, and figured if we could afford the gas, we stimulated the economy by consuming it.

As if that didn't already make us all complicit in contributing to global warming, to live well we came to think we needed daily newspapers (growing ever thicker with ad supplements), weekly magazines and paper for our computers—which were *supposed* to reduce our need for paper. I subscribe to *Newberg Graphic*, a small-town newspaper that comes twice a week, *Newsweek* and *Books and Culture*. I am complicit in the use of trees.

Exotic woods like Brazilian cherry became the new best look for floors and kitchen cabinets, and we needed more of the regular stuff—the spruce, pine and fir—to build our bigger homes. We cleared forests to create pasture to graze cows for six months before they were sent off for fattening up at the CAFO, and we cleared forests so we could grow corn to fatten the cows once they got there.

Let's shorten this long disheartening story: what causes global warming? One answer says it is an unavoidable natural shift in earth's orbit and axis. A second answer says it's the high carbon lifestyle of affluent humans and nations and the increasing numbers of humans and nations achieving affluence. This is shifting the balance of earth's atmosphere so that we unleash more greenhouse gases than are absorbed, resulting in a feedback loop that has set a small but significant warming trend that is destabilizing our world's climate.

### What's so destabilizing about a small warm-up?

When I first heard about global warming I lived in Chicago and thought a bit of warming could be a good thing—at least for Chicagoans in winter. So what if earth's temperature has increased one degree Fahrenheit since 1970? Can it be such a terrible thing for thaws to come a week earlier to the Arctic and freezes to begin a week later? Has anyone polled the people living in Alaska to ask them if *they* mind?

Global warming isn't the best term to use for what we're experiencing; it's not broad enough in scope. Global climate change is better, and climate instability better yet. Those of us living in the Northern Hemisphere won't be affected much for a while, but climate-change effects are already being significantly felt in other parts of the world. The Arctic is affected the most, and that matters to all of us because the ice caps reflect a lot of the sun's rays back into space. Remember those pictures of earth taken from the Apollo missions in the 1970s? Ice caps covered the North and South Poles. With the Arctic ice having shrunk 25 percent since then, by 2040 (much sooner by some accounts) it will have its first ice-free summer, which, however good that sounds, is actually *not* something to celebrate. Glaciers and mountain snowcaps are melting too. Montana's Glacier National Park now has twenty-seven glaciers. In 1910 it had 150.

This may be stating the obvious, but as ice melts there is less of it to reflect the sun's rays back into space, which means more of it melts. This rather efficient ice-melting feedback loop not only warms the oceans but also releases methane gas—a greenhouse

gas that had been stored under frozen ice since the last ice age—
into the atmosphere.

That's a sampling of what's happening. How that impacts earth's
inhabitants can be put into two general categories, related to the
shifting of earth's water. One impact is felt in areas that get more
water than they can handle, and a second in areas that lose water
necessary to sustain life.

*A cup of water.* Most of us have heard that melting ice caps are
causing sea levels to rise, somewhere between seven and twenty-
three inches. I didn't understand why a few inches of water was
such a big deal; can't folks just build their sandcastles and homes
a few feet farther inland? Then I learned that a four-inch rise will
flood many South Sea Islands and swamp much of Southeast Asia,
resulting in the migration of people inland, and in some cases, a
complete transplanting of cultures and people. Due to its geographic location, Bangladesh has already experienced ten years of
devastating flooding, and is one of the most vulnerable nations to
the effects of climate change. Up to twenty-five million people
may be displaced in the next couple of decades. The nine coral
atolls south of the equator that make up the country of Tuvalu, the
smallest country in the world outside of the Vatican, will disappear under water and the entire population of eleven thousand
will need to be transplanted elsewhere. The people of Tuvalu and
Bangladesh are not contributing to global warming by burning
fossil fuels, but they're facing the consequences of sharing a planet
with those of us who do. At the UN General Assembly in 2003 the
prime minister of Tuvalu, Saufatu Sopoanga, said,

> We live in constant fear of the adverse impacts of climate
> change. For a coral atoll nation, sea level rise and more se-
> vere weather events loom as a growing threat to our entire
> population. The threat is real and serious, and is of no differ-
> ence to a slow and insidious form of terrorism against us.

People from places as diverse as Vietnam and Louisiana will be displaced. In addition, where ecosystems are destroyed in the ice caps and coastal regions, plants, insects and animals that are particular to those areas and cannot migrate will die.

The "too little" water problem comes from glaciers disappearing in areas depending on mountain snows for spring, summer and fall water. These areas are experiencing and will increasingly experience water shortages and drought. Aquifers are drying up and deserts are expanding, driving people and animals that can migrate off their lands and into increasingly crowded neighboring ones, and killing off species that can't.

Our capacity to grow food will decline, leading to more severe global food shortages. If that's not bad enough news, the decreased presence of water and increasing global temperatures will make drought, heat waves and wildfires more commonplace everywhere. Biologists studying climate change predict that 30 percent of all species will become extinct as their habitat disappears and the ecosystem that sustains them changes. This is happening in sub-Saharan Africa, where expanding deserts, drought and increasing food shortages already compromise the well-being of Africa's people and creatures.

Will humanity survive? I'm not hearing anyone saying we won't. Fewer of us may inhabit the planet, which is probably a good thing for the other creatures trying to make a go of it for themselves and their offspring. Plants, insects, animals and people in the next century will have migrated a bit inland and away from expanding desert regions. Life will be around for some time yet—but it will not be the same planet that we experience now. That is a dire picture. If humans are causing climate change, we ought to step back and reconsider the life we have crafted for ourselves and its impact on others.

If climate change is a natural turn of events, then I could call it the hand of God and not feel one tad bit responsible. Besides, this scenario sounds like something from a science fiction apocalyptic movie. Sometimes I feel like scoffing at the whole thing and wonder if I'm a bit dimwitted to be taking these fantastic claims about climate change seriously. I could choose to simply hope that things will turn out okay, which is decidedly easier than trying to figure out what it means to walk gently in this dismal picture. What can any one person do anyway?

I still stand by what I said at the beginning: taking global warming seriously does *not* require a complete overhaul of our lifestyle. Making changes is less disruptive than we fear. It *will* require revisiting what we think about economic growth and progress and our sense of entitlement. For instance, we will need to be willing to stop building more coal-burning energy plants and invest instead in the renewable energy alternatives already available. I join those who are convinced that there is a way out of this, even if the way out requires political will to change international policies. I am optimistic because the political winds are shifting.

## WHAT'S THE GLOBAL RESPONSE TO GLOBAL WARMING?

On October 24, 2009, the world experienced its first International Day of Climate Action, which raised public awareness and called for a global climate treaty. People and organizations around the world expressed their commitment to establishing a more sustainable future by planning activities and creating gigantic "350" signs, of which they then sent pictures to 350.org to be linked with others and uploaded for display at Times Square in New York City. People used kayaks on rivers, bicycles, people, trash and tents to make their "350" signs, representing a world united in the goal to bring down our level of carbon dioxide in the atmosphere.

A democracy is based on the assumption that if the masses speak, leaders will listen. They are listening already. Leaders of the world know that we want them to take aggressive steps to effectively bring an international response to climate change, to lower carbon emissions to a level that can sustain the kind of world we were born into.

The willingness to revisit some assumptions is at the crux of this crisis. The biggest challenge is to get the world's leaders to heed the scientific community and make commitments to cut national carbon emissions. For the sake of consistency I need to ask if I am willing to cut my own. As a Christian this is a moral question. If I am to love my neighbor, be a steward of creation and represent God on earth, then I have an obligation to consider that human activity might be negatively impacting earth and to be willing to see what I can do to minimize the harm. A love of justice and desire for *shalom* flow from a life of prayer, Bible reading, study and meditation. As God's agents in the world, we can offer hope and partner with God in bringing about the redemption for which creation groans. Especially when we act together.

Even if climate change is inevitable, I would rather err on the side of activity that seeks the good of creation, rather than inactivity driven by either fatalism (I can't do anything about it anyway) or skepticism (I haven't been convinced I'm contributing to a problem). What if something *can* be done, but we choose not to act because *maybe* nothing can be done? I choose to live as an optimist. We can make different choices.

The good news (and there is much good news) is that a lot is already being done, and we can join efforts already underway to lessen our own carbon footprint, and that of our communities, our country and our world, which is the focus of the next chapter.

Another bit of good news is that we have acted effectively as a global community before. We used to send a lot of synthetic gases up in the air, until we realized that a number of them were destroying the ozone layer that, among other things, protected us from the sun's ultraviolet rays. CFCs (chlorofluorocarbon) and other ozone-depleting substances were in our Styrofoam cups, packaging, aerosol cans, and refrigerator and air-conditioner coolants. Climatologists watching the ozone layer depletion eventually got the world's attention, and in 1987 the Montreal Protocol reflected the agreement of nations to phase out CFCs and other ozone-depleting chemicals. The UN secretary general at the time, Kofi Annan, said the effort was "perhaps the single most successful international agreement to date." Human action brought about a global response to fix a problem we created. Given our world's culture clashes, civil wars and general distrust of each other, this is an amazing accomplishment.

Since the global oil crisis and recession of the 1970s, leaders of some of the most powerful nations have come together annually to talk about global issues like the world economy, Africa and development, the environment and climate change. Currently the members of this group, referred to as the G8, are Canada, France, Germany, Italy, Japan, Russia, the United Kingdom, the United States and the president of the European Commission, though leaders of other countries are occasionally invited to participate. At the 2009 G8 Summit, the United States, Japan, Russia and Canada agreed with the European Union to implement policy changes aimed at limiting the global temperature increase to two degrees Celsius, requiring cutting carbon emissions by 80 percent. Global leaders are setting national objectives and mid-term goals to create accountability to insure this is not merely a conversation but a commitment for change. In December 2009, a world climate-change conference was held in Copenhagen, where world leaders worked out new protocols, agreements to collectively work to check climate change given the data and the fact that the Kyoto Protocol was due to expire in 2012.

Perhaps the ozone layer depletion challenge a decade ago was our trial run, a warm-up exercise for a task that will be more complex and will affect how we think about development and do agriculture, forestry, transportation, and all kinds of industry and manufacturing.

Lester Brown, president of Earth Policy Institute, sets forth a plan to help us rethink those areas. *Plan B* is an aggressive program to mobilize the planet to respond to global climage change. Plan A, by the way, is to continue living as we do now, to hunt down new sources of fossil fuels, and to foster growth and development for all so that every family can drive two or three cars, live in air-conditioned homes, eat meat daily (or more than once a day), and travel the globe for business and pleasure.

China offers one example of the unsustainability of Plan A. China now consumes more of the world's basic resources than we do in the United States—and we are big resource consumers. China is growing and developing at a phenomenal rate and is predicted to "catch up" to the West by 2030, meaning their income per person will match ours in the West. If China acquires cars at the same rate we do, which is three cars for every four people, China will use more barrels of oil per day to fuel cars than is being produced worldwide. Plan A will lead to failure. We have to turn things around. Brown says we need economists to start thinking like ecologists, as well as leaders who can understand how the economy and economic growth are intrinsically linked to earth's systems that support us and make life possible.

To implement Plan B requires leaders of the world to address three goals simultaneously. One is to eradicate poverty, which doesn't, on first pass, seem all that connected to climate change. But we can't turn things around without addressing global poverty. Widespread poverty is associated with a nation's fragility. When nation-states fail, governments lose control of their territory and people. Disorder threatens to unravel society, and civil wars erupt as tribal groups, street gangs or organized crime groups vie for control of power and resources. Basic services like education, healthcare and the availability of food falter, or disappear altogether. In an effort to gain political advantage, groups at war seldom count the cost of destroying ecosystems. The destruction of forests, grassland deterioration, soil erosion, and the shrinking of available crop land and water per person are linked to fragile and failed states. This is why eradicating poverty is one of Lester Brown's three goals to save civilization and the planet. The United Nations shares that goal, and the Millennial Development Goals (MDGs) set by the UN have made progress in the first nine years of the century.

Brown's second goal is to stabilize the world's population, a topic that will be addressed in a future chapter, and the third is restoring earth's natural systems. This part of his plan involves cutting carbon dioxide emissions by 80 percent by 2020, a more rigorous goal than the 2009 G8 Summit commitment to cut emissions by 80 percent for industrialized countries and 50 percent globally by 2050. Brown outlines the cost, compares it to what we spend on other federal budget lines and makes it seem possible.

Cutting carbon dioxide emissions doesn't primarily come from all of us driving less, eating less meat and turning more lights off—though that is part of the solution. More significantly the solution comes from raising energy efficiency so that we require less to run our various machines and lights, developing renewable sources of energy so that we use and rely on less fossil fuel, and planting trees while banning deforestation. In each of these areas change is underway. New sources of energy and our use of it is discussed in the next chapter. But be encouraged—the conversation has been going on for some time, and corporations, hospitals, churches, universities, and whole cities, counties and countries are on board, cutting their carbon footprint in an effort to become low carbon communities. Examples help me see what's possible and keep the whole of it from being so overwhelming. So here's one story—to balance out some of the despair over what all needs to be done.

*A simple idea.* Matt Prescott, an environmental consultant from the U.K. and director of the Ban the Bulb campaign, came up with a simple idea. He started an online movement in 2006 to ban incandescent light bulbs in the U.K., a simple change that could have a significant impact on climate change. In a few years no one would miss incandescent bulbs anymore. Who misses aerosol hairspray cans taken out of production to stop ozone layer damage? The bulbs would be replaced with compact fluorescent (CFL) ones or light-emitting diodes (LED), some of which have been on the market for thirty years and have been improved significantly along the way. These bulbs use five times less energy, and contribute 60 to 70 percent *less* to greenhouse gases.

The U.K. signed on, as well as other European countries and European bulb manufacturers. In 2008 the United States passed its own national plan to ban incandescent bulbs by 2012, although fifteen states had already passed or considered legislation to restrict or ban traditional bulbs. Energy companies throughout the nation are offering incentives to encourage residents to exchange incandescent bulbs for CFL bulbs. Even small electric companies are part of the effort. In 2009 the Forest Grove Power and Light Company gave away up to twenty CFL light bulbs per family to local residents. Since lighting accounts for about 20 percent of a home's energy use, this is a significant move on behalf of electric companies. If each of us in the United States replaced just one incandescent bulb with a CFL bulb, in a year's time we would save enough energy to light more than three million homes *and* we'd keep the equivalent of 800,000 cars' worth of carbon dioxide out of the atmosphere. That one change does the world a significant bit of good.

More energy-efficient features are making their way into houses, office complexes, schools, hospitals and stores. The answer to global warming is not to return to an age where we didn't have electricity, but to become more thoughtful and intentional about how we use it, and to replace our dependence on fossil fuel for energy with renewable sources.

*Planting trees while banning deforestation.* Any conversation about global warming or the global environmental and ecological issues will involve forests. Deforestation is a global concern; it's not quite like there are *our* forests and *their* forests—we're all dependent on the well-being of earth's forests.

If you asked me what we use trees for more than anything else, I would have said either for building or to make paper. If you asked a woman from Africa what trees get used for more than anything else she'd probably say for fuel, particularly to cook food. She'd be right and I'd be wrong. Around the world trees are used for fuel more than for any other purpose, accounting for a little more than half of all trees cut down from earth's forests.

That's not to say recycling paper isn't important. If we all recycled paper as effectively as South Korea (77 percent of their paper gets recycled), the amount of trees needed to produce paper would drop by a third. We're putting more focus on reducing our use of paper products that only get used once—like shopping bags, which you may get to start paying for if you choose to use them rather than bring your own. Cloth napkins are making a comeback, as are cloth diapers, replacing the particularly troubling disposable product that became popular thirty years ago, filling our landfills with a mixture of plastics, paper and poop.

There is good news on the forest front. Rocket stoves in sub-Saharan Africa and solar cookers in Kenya are examples of projects aimed at replacing burning trees with sustainable alternatives like biomass or solar energy for cooking food. The stoves improve air quality, decrease carbon dioxide emissions and save forests.

Meanwhile global efforts are protecting earth's forests. Some are being preserved for the important rich biodiversity they hold, and others are being managed in sustainable ways, where harvesting corresponds with replanting. The European Union has good reason to feel optimistic about meeting their Kyoto Protocol agreement goals. In addition to technologies that are minimizing greenhouse gases, they are expanding their forests. A University of Helsinki study found that between 1990 and 2005, the expansion of forests in the EU countries absorbed an additional 126 million tons of carbon every year, equal to 11 percent of Europe's total emissions. Trees are capturing and storing more carbon than researchers expected, and Europe's forests are thriving and will be significant in helping Europe meet its environmental goals.

Reducing the net loss of trees around the world to zero, so that no more trees are cut down than are planted, is the goal set by the World Wildlife Fund (WWF), and they hope to achieve it by 2020. The goal involves partnering with government, civil society and the business sector to support sustainable use of forests, reverse forest loss, and increase both the quality and quantity of forests.

Global and corporate actions are lightening our carbon footprint. If we choose to participate, we will be joining movements already underway. Mark and I are trying to do our part by regrowing a forest where we live. For the last twenty years or so this land had been a pasture for cows. We've planted more than 750 fir, cedar and pine seedlings in the last three years, and two dozen fruit trees besides. Our spirits lighten as we tend our young forest and orchard. Almost anyone can plant a tree somewhere. And every tree helps more than you'd imagine. Individual effort is important, as it will be individuals working together to inspire churches and communities to challenge energy companies, members of Congress and world leaders to bring about change.

Christians have come on board. We are joining movements like the Evangelical Environmental Network and Restoring Eden: Christians for Environmental Stewardship. As of 2009 more than 260 senior evangelical Christian leaders from the United States had signed The Evangelical Climate Initiative. Signers include pastors like Rick Warren, Bill Hybels and Rob Bell; college and university presidents; Leith Anderson, president of the National Association of Evangelicals (NAE); David Neff, editor in chief of *Christianity Today*; Dr. Timothy George, dean and professor of divinity at Beeson Divinity School; and leaders of organizations like the Salvation Army and World Relief. Together they are declaring a commitment to work toward a sustainable future by reducing carbon dioxide emissions in their organizations. The movement is inspiring Christians in churches, on college campuses and in various organizations to embrace God's creation, to take seriously the task of being stewards and to work toward global change.

A sustainable path is emerging that will allow for the flourishing of future generations of polar bears, salmon, salamanders, owls, hummingbirds and bees. And humans too. It will allow our children, grandchildren and great-grandchildren to flourish in a world striving toward greater health and wholeness.

o   o   o

## RESOURCES

*Where can I read more on climate change?*

- For a great, clever, ten-minute video produced by a science teacher that looks at the logic behind the choices we have ahead of us, go to <www.youtube.com/wonderingmind42>.

- 350.org is working globally to raise awareness and gather voices to speak to world leaders about climate change. The website is full of various kinds of information—from background knowledge to how to get involved.

  *2150 Allston Way, Suite 340*
  *The David Brower Center*
  *Berkeley, CA 94704*
  *Phone: (510) 250-7860*

- Pew Center on Global Climate Change. The center "brings together business leaders, policy makers, scientists, and other experts to bring a new approach to a complex and often controversial issue. Our approach is based on sound science, straight talk, and a belief that we can work together to protect the climate while sustaining economic growth."

  *2101 Wilson Blvd., Suite 550*
  *Arlington, VA 22201*
  *Phone: (703) 516-4146*
  *www.pewclimate.org/global-warming-basics/online_resources*

*How can I learn about energy rebates on light bulbs (and other rebates) in my area?*

- If you live in the northwest go to <www.northwestenergystar.com/partner-resources/incentives/index.php?state=OR&utility=ALL&incentives=Bulbs>.

- For federal rebates on a number of different appliances and energy-using products see <www.energystar.gov/index.cfm?c=tax_credits.tx_index>.

*How can I learn more about reforestation and reforestation projects?*

- Carbonfund is a non-profit provider of carbon offsets and attempts to make it "easy and affordable for any individual, business or organization to reduce & offset their climate impact and [hasten] the transformation to a clean energy future."

  *1320 Fenwick Lane, Suite 206*
  *Silver Spring, MD 20910*
  *Phone: (240) 247-0630*
  *www.carbonfund.org/site/pages/our_projects/category/Reforestation/*

- If you want to join a reforestation project go to <www.charityguide.org/volunteer/vacation/deforestation-reforestation.htm>.

***How can I learn more about the green job industry and green jobs that are available?***

- The two organizations below are online agencies that help connect employers and job seekers to green job industries.

  *Great Green Careers*
  *1503 SW 42nd St.*
  *Topeka, KS 66609-1265*
  *www.greatgreencareers.com*

  *Green Jobs*
  *P.O. Box 916*
  *Fairfield, CA 94533*
  *Phone: (707) 434-9201*
  *www.greenjobs.com*

***What are some Christian environmental organizations?***

- The Cornwall Alliance is "a coalition of clergy, theologians, religious leaders, scientists, academics, and policy experts committed to bringing a balanced Biblical view of stewardship to issues of environment and development."

  *www.cornwallalliance.org/about/*

- Evangelical Environmental Network is "a non-profit organization that seeks to educate, inspire, and mobilize Christians in their effort to care for God's creation, to be faithful stewards of God's provision, and to advocate for actions and policies that honor God and protect the environment."

  *680 I Street SW*
  *Washington, DC 20024*
  *Phone: (202) 903-0209*
  *www.creationcare.org/*

- Evangelicals for Social Action is "an association of Christians seeking to promote Christian engagement, analysis and understanding of major social, cultural and public policy issues." Creation care is one of their focus points.

*The Sider Center on Ministry and Public Policy*
*6 E. Lancaster Ave.*
*Wynnewood, PA 19096-3420*
*Phone: (484) 384-2990*
*www.esa-online.org/Display.asp?Page=creationcare*

- Not One Sparrow: A Christian Voice for Animals
  *www.notonesparrow.com/*

- Restoring Eden: Christians for Environmental Stewardship
  *http://restoringeden.org*

# PRELUDE

## The Earth Has Weight

*Asase ye duru*

In college I started reading *A History of Celibacy* by Elizabeth Abbott. Starting with the Greek goddess Athena and continuing into modern times it tells the stories of those who chose a life of celibacy. For some reason, which took me a while to figure out, I always happened to pick up this book around the two-month mark of a new relationship (which may have contributed to the demise of several college relationships). Dedicating the totality of my life to something great has always appealed to me. I often thought of surrendering the luxury of love so that I might go live in the Red Light District in Bangkok, work in a hospice center or build a farmhouse in Malawi with doors wide open to all children. If you had asked me if I would choose a life of celibacy to care for the earth I probably would have laughed at you, claiming I'd much rather be helping people than saving forests.

Oh, the realizations that have bombarded me since those early college days! For starters, although it may be harder, I've decided it is still quite possible to dedicate the totality of one's life to something great *even* if married. In fact, marriage and family might be the very venue through which certain services are rendered. A second humbling realization was that a life dedicated to the earth is a life well lived. A life dedicated to God's creation is a life dedicated to loving one's neighbor. I used to laugh at my environmentalist sisters and mother, proudly proclaiming, "I'd rather take care of a person than a tree." I had yet to realize that I could not possibly take care of a person without consideration of the tree, for indeed it is all interconnected.

In the fall of 2007 I went to a conference hosted by Micah Challenge, a Christian campaign to end poverty, and the National Association of Evangelicals. I listened to evangelical leaders discuss their concern for the environment as they proclaimed that the climate was one of the most pressing issues for the church, that this was one of the greatest *human* rights issues, because climate change causes less rainfall and thus greater famine.

Famine is a face I know well. In 2005 I worked with World Relief in Malawi, a country struggling under the weight of a long dry season and a shorter rainy season than usual. Half the population was considered to be starving. Rice became more expensive, *kasava* rare, malnourished children common. I watched as the cradles in the Crisis Nursery Center in Lilongwe quickly filled up to capacity. This was the second serious famine in just a matter of years; the rainy season is becoming shorter and less predictable, and much of the country still lacks irrigation infrastructure, leaving Malawians at the mercy of rain. If the way I live impacts the rain in this area, surely ecology is a human rights issue. This is a cause worth living for.

As a lifelong Protestant, I find encouragement from my Roman Catholic sisters—especially those known as the Green Sisters. Sarah McFarland Taylor, author of *Green Sisters,* says: "When orphanages were needed in North America, religious sisters' communities built orphanages. When hospitals were needed, sisters built hospitals and staffed them. When schools were needed, sisters built schools and taught in them." When the poor cry out for justice the Sisters of Charity provide human dignity to the dying and marginalized. Throughout history the monastic tradition has met societies' urgent needs. Today, "Green Sisters" continue that tradition as they gather around the needs of earth, responding to creation's cries. The Green Sisters are the new "missionaries to the planet."

Green Sisters build and work in contemplative gardens. They use their communal lands in ecologically sustainable ways. In rural areas Green Sisters engage in conserving farmland and farming in sustainable ways. In suburban areas they work to preserve public space and help communities become self-sufficient, and in urban areas they plant community gardens as a tangible way to address issues of poverty and hunger. As they preserve land and live sustainably on it, they simultaneously feed the hungry by supplying soup kitchens with fresh fruit and vegetables, and providing jobs for the homeless.

The evangelical church often has ministries that mirror monastic orders: ministries reaching into inner cities and ghettos, mission trips, food pantries, prayer meetings. Where the Catholic Church has orders, the evangelical church has programs. However, we've yet to see many "green programs."

I wonder if this is lacking because it does not feel like a noble task. Helping with Katrina relief or AIDS work—now *that* is noble. I admit in the big scheme of things caring for creation doesn't *feel* as urgent, but it is. The Green Sisters understand that loving others is intertwined with loving the earth. As Sister Elizabeth Walters from Hope Takes Root, an urban garden that pays people that are homeless to plant, said, "If we look out for the Earth, we're looking out for each other."

All environmental actions are meaningful. They can thrust the world toward abundant life or push it toward droughts followed

by famines. We cannot differentiate between care for our neighbors and care for the earth. The Ghanaian symbol *Asase ye duru*
("the Earth has weight") represents the importance of the earth in
sustaining life. The proverb associated with this symbol is *"Asase
ye duru se po,"* translated "the earth is heavier than the sea." This
metaphor reminds us that it is earth that sustains our very life.
The earth is the source of life. A call to ecological sustainability is
not simply due to love for earth because it is God's creation, but
also because earth is the sustainer of life. To watch over earth is to
watch over that which sustains life. Christians value life. This is at
the heart of our theology; Christ came to give life and to give it
abundantly.

Central to my understanding of the Christian mission are Jesus' words, "I came that they may have life and have it abundantly"
(John 10:10 ESV). *Asase ye duru* helps me to understand I cannot
give life in abundance to my neighbors if I am not contributing to
the well-being of that which sustains us all.

*The History of Celibacy* sits on my bookshelf. It has not been
opened in a while, which is probably good for the sake of my marriage. I still get aches, though, when I read about a young American midwife in Malawi, or a friend who is working in Thailand.
For now, the reality of student loans keeps me from a "romantic"
life overseas. I am trying to figure out how to live well in the context of marriage, routine and regularity. Do I take the extra fifteen
minutes to hang the laundry on the line to dry? Do I eat less chocolate chip cookies so I can actually afford the eight dollars a pound
for fair-trade chocolate? Do I take the half-eaten veggie burger in
the oversized to-go box? These questions aren't very romantic or
exciting, but they are the questions that make up the backbone of
our daily lives. These are the questions that, if unasked, may fill
up our dumps and harm our life-sustaining earth.

# FUELS THAT FIRE
# OUR ENGINES

*Let me break it down for you.*
*People don't want to sit in the dark for an hour in 2009. Period.*

—JOHN COLE, FROM A PERSONAL BLOG

On March 31, 2007, Sydney, Australia, held the first Earth Hour, encouraging inhabitants of Sydney to turn out lights in their homes, businesses and civic gathering places for an hour. Over two million people participated, and the energy saved was equivalent to shutting down twelve coal plants for an hour. The next year Earth Hour went global, and 50 million people from 370 cities in 35 different countries shut off their lights for an hour, including U.S. cities like Atlanta, Phoenix and Chicago, and places as diverse as Rome, Manila and Tel Aviv. According to the Earth Hour Media Centre, on March 28, 2009, hundreds of millions of people "voted earth" in the world's largest show of public concern over climate change. Apparently folks *did* want to sit in the dark for an hour. People from over three thousand cities and towns in eighty-three countries participated in the third, and now annual, global demonstration.

Also in 2009 the Obama administration made a commitment to fight global warming, setting a goal of reducing U.S. carbon emissions by 20 percent by 2020 (bringing them back to 1990 levels), and reducing carbon emissions by 80 percent by 2050. Members of some industries think this is unrealistically rigorous; leaders from other countries committed to the same or higher cuts themselves do not think it is rigorous enough. While that gets figured out in the political and economic realms, we can add our voice to the global community that is scrutinizing how much fossil fuel our lifestyle requires to move matter that matters to us (food and stuff), and to light, warm and run the motors and circuitry boards in our homes.

## HOW SHALL WE THEN LIVE?

Owning a hot tub is an inconsistency in my life—a life otherwise characterized by opening and closing windows for summer breezes, raising and lowering shades against the summer sun, and using ceiling fans instead of the air conditioner. My efforts to conserve are sometimes a bit over-the-top (or a lot of times over-the-top, depending on who is recording it). I think my family members find it especially annoying when I go behind them, turning off lights as they leave a room.

Donna and Bob, my generous in-laws, gave us the hot tub after deciding they weren't using it enough to merit having it anymore, and I'm beginning to wonder if we should pass it on to someone else. I do realize that giving it away doesn't reduce the use of energy overall, even if it reduces *my* use of energy, and this awareness troubles me. However, when dampness settles into my bones during the dark chill of Oregon's winter days, I relish the ability to end my day by slipping into the hot tub. I check to be sure the winter constellations are still in the right places and listen to critters that break through winter's quiet while warmth penetrates through the day's busyness and demands all the way to my bones. I sleep particularly well on such nights.

But last July I realized we had been heating water for some weeks in a hot tub that hadn't been used by anyone—not even our children, who stayed with us at various points throughout the summer. The time had come to unplug and empty it.

You may empathize with my situation. I want to be a good citizen of earth and of God's kingdom, to love my neighbor as I love myself. At the same time I want to revel in the wonder and beauty of a life that God meant to be abundant. When does denial of all convenience and comfort reflect a gnostic view of the body, one that sees all bodily pleasures as a block to spiritual maturity and so refuses to sip and savor the good of creation, comfort and creativity? When is too much comfort and convenience hard to justify? I'm struggling to find a balance that embraces some of the comforts we've invented along the way, while questioning others. I want to learn to walk gently with grace, gratitude and humility through the struggle.

Sometimes my response has been to condemn all energy-using devises—to try to emulate modern-day prophets like Wendell Berry who live as lightly as possible on the land, using as little energy as possible. Berry knows that the bulk of his region's energy comes from leveling and destroying the Appalachian Mountains for coal, so he uses horses instead of a tractor and lanterns instead of electric lights, and seldom accepts invitations to fly across the country to speak. I'm not quite there. For one thing, I don't own horses. And I use lights, a computer and a car. It isn't very productive to live paralyzed by guilt for the energy I use, but I still welcome the struggle and appreciate Berry's prophetic voice. I want to be as thoughtful in my choices as Berry is with his.

So I set out to learn what I could about our country's dependence on foreign oil, where we get the electricity that fuels our nation, and what we as individuals and communities can do to step into the green energy movement. One inspiring tidbit I learned along the way was that most of our homes were built to meet *mini-*

*mum* standards of energy efficiency, so even if we think we have efficient homes, we can all do something to help lighten our use of resources and save money on our utility bills. Some of the simple changes hardly affect our lives at all but, when combined with individuals in our communities, states and nation doing the same, can reduce our collective demand for energy significantly.

Mark and I are making progress, seeking to reduce our use of energy bit by bit and to replace fossil-based energy with renewable, or green, sources of energy. In the process we're choosing with intention which comforts and conveniences to keep, and which to give up.

## THE HOME AUDIT

Mark built our home in the middle of a pasture that we've now replanted in forest—our toddler trees, we call them, that are stretching toward adolescence. From our back porch and patio we can look into the old forest that remains. Oak, maple, cedar and fir trees shade and draw life from a little creek. We refer to this place as "Fern Creek" because ferns flourish in the dappled shade alongside the creek and throughout the bit of forest that remains. More importantly, calling this place "Fern Creek" keeps us from referring to it as "our property," which sounds presumptuous.

We wanted to build a home with as much attention to walking gently as we could. So we used engineered lumber in our framing, and Trex, a recycled plastic decking material that never needs painting or replacing, for porches and outside stairs. We put CFL light bulbs throughout our home, used an environmentally friendly paint (no-VOC paint), and heat and cool our home with a geothermal system that gives us hot water as a free byproduct of the heating and cooling process. We have Energy Star appliances and thermal pane windows, and used bamboo for flooring, wool carpet in the basement and sisal wool area rugs. Our kitchen cabinets were made from wood off an old onion barn in the little town of Gaston a few miles down the road, and the furnishings with the most character in our home are those passed down to us through family, or picked up and reclaimed secondhand.

We didn't do everything possible to make our home ecologically sound, and some of our choices are a toss-up in terms of benefit and cost. We're not sure we'd choose bamboo for flooring again. Bamboo is a sustainable product; it's a grass that replenishes itself in six to eight years, so it's a more sustainable choice than the slow-growing oak tree. But it still took a chunk of fossil fuel to get it shipped across the ocean (which means Brazilian cherry and other exotic woods are a costly environmental choice because of both transportation and sustainable growth issues). Maybe a faster-growing local wood, such as maple, would have been a better choice, or investing in reclaimed wood flooring, something akin to the wood used for our kitchen cabinets. We did a fair bit to attend to walking gently, but we could have done more.

We hope to install solar panels on our south-facing roof eventually. Until we get those up and running, Mark and I still use a fair amount of electricity that comes from burning coal. A home audit helped in figuring out how we might shave off some of the greenhouse gases we release into the atmosphere every day. There are different options for home audits, depending on how specific you want to get. You can hire an energy rater who will come in and do a comprehensive audit of your home. You can also purchase an electricity-reading meter that can be plugged into any appliance to measure the electricity use of that appliance and help you compute almost exactly how much carbon dioxide your lifestyle emits month by month. Appendix A offers an example of what a home audit might look like.

The average person in the United States emits about twenty tons of carbon dioxide into the atmosphere per year. That is more than twice what Brits (nine tons) and the French (six tons) emit—who have collectively worked hard to decrease carbon dioxide emissions in the last decade. People in Honduras and India emit about a ton per year, and while China only emits four tons per person now, that number is rising rapidly with China's rising standard of living. To put this in perspective, the global average is between four and five tons per person. So decreasing our individual carbon emissions is a good opportunity to aim low, to shoot for being below average.

## THINKING OUTSIDE THE HOUSE

Decreasing your use of hot water, installing ceiling fans and CFL light bulbs, hanging clothes out to dry, recycling—all these use less energy. But discovering ways to reduce carbon dioxide emissions gets more creative than that. Planting a maple tree that provides shade for the western or southern part of your home will cut down your use of summer air conditioning, delight you with red, orange or yellow leaves in the fall, *and* start absorbing carbon dioxide from the get-go, helping offset some of your home's carbon emissions. Plant trees. They absorb carbon dioxide from the atmosphere and effectively store it for us all.

Enticements for putting solar panels on our rooftops are coming from both state and federal sources. Currently in Oregon a sixteen-thousand-dollar system would cost a thousand dollars after the state and federal tax incentives. Incentives like this, which only work for U.S. citizens who make enough money to pay significant taxes, reflect an awareness that the burden for investing in green energy rightfully falls more heavily on the shoulders of those more able to afford it. Perhaps there is a greater responsibility for those with higher incomes to help our communities, states and nation more quickly transition from fossil-fuel sources to sustainable green ones. While most of us can afford CFL bulbs, some of us can afford more expensive options.

If you have a boiler and need to replace it, consider buying one fueled by biomass. If you need to replace a furnace and live in a moderate climate, consider getting a heat pump. If you live in a rural area, be the first in the neighborhood to set up a wind turbine. If you put it in your vegetable garden, the wind turbine becomes a multiuse investment—energy producer, tall garden sculpture and scarecrow!

It's also possible to use renewable energy without bringing it directly into your home or yard. Individuals and businesses in most states can pay a little more each month to purchase renewable power. By paying more per kilowatt-hour for energy, you join local efforts to help your electrical company invest in green energy, making it possible for companies to invest in and build green energy alternatives that lower your state's dependence on fossil fuels, like coal. As of 2008, almost seventy thousand customers in Oregon had signed onto the Portland General Electric (PGE) residential renewable power program, which put PGE first in the nation for customer support of renewable energy for four consecutive years. According to PGE, those customers are supporting wind farms in the Northwest and the development of other green energy sources, and in 2008 collectively kept more than 622 million pounds of carbon dioxide from the air, which is the same as taking about 55,350 cars off the road for a year.

It's not just residents helping change the air quality in Oregon. So is Burgerville, a regional fast-food franchise, along with the cities of Beaverton, Hillsboro and Gresham, the Oregon Health Sciences University, and Lewis and Clark College. All of these have chosen to fuel their city governments, businesses or schools with clean wind power from PGE. We have the technology to lower our dependence on fossil fuels by shifting to renewable sources. We are finding the will.

Anyone can look up energy sources for their state on the Internet and learn what their city, county and state are up to, and what collective efforts they might join. Information and inspiration is at our fingertips. We walk more gently and leave a sustainable future for our children's children as we learn about renewable energy sources, and support city, county and state development of green energy.

We also walk more gently by using less. I need to keep asking myself to differentiate between the energy I *need* and my use of energy from habit or because I like the convenience and comfort of it. When I stop to critique my energy use, it alters the way I see myself in the world. I realize I don't need nearly as much energy as I've come accustomed to using.

If we look at our energy-use choices with the desire to foster the flourishing of life everywhere, our choices become easier to make. When that not-yet-imagined energy solution becomes available, then using less won't be as important, but we're not having that conversation yet—because only a small percent of our energy comes from renewable sources. At the December 2009 Copenhagen Climate Conference, the United States joined other nations in declaring a desire to be responsible world citizens. This commitment represents a bottom-up, or grass-roots, movement that has inspired individuals, companies, cities, states and the nation to act.

We can join the challenge by forming a group with other families in support of change. Share ideas and resources. Challenge each other to cut 10 percent of your energy bills for the next year and talk about how you are doing it. Start a committee to look into energy/resource use at your workplace or church. Or implement a Voluntary Gas Tithe, like a member of our church did. Participants track their gas purchases and every month give a tithe of what they spend filling up their cars back to the church which we then use for projects to "green" up our church and to provide weatherizing for low-income residents in our community.

The writer of Hebrews encourages us to spur each other on to love and good works (Hebrews 10:24). We are social creatures and almost always handle changes more easily in the context of church and community. Others encourage, inspire, hold us accountable and broaden the spectrum of possibility.

## NEW BURSTS OF ENERGY: THE PATH TO ALTERNATIVE SUSTAINABLE ENERGY

We encountered train traffic when we moved to the suburbs of Chicago. Trains came and went into the city all day long, rumbling across our suburban streets. We'd stop at the tracks and watch them going into and coming out of Chicago; often the ones going in were loaded with car after car of coal. I didn't know what Chicago did with it all. Did people still heat their homes and businesses by burning coal in furnaces? Coming from Oregon, where trains and coal were both scarce, I didn't actually know that *electricity* comes from burning coal—including *my* electricity. I must have missed that lesson somewhere in the fourth or fifth grade.

Understanding where our nation's energy comes from is part of the conversation, and some of you are more interested in it than others. I've provided another primer of sorts, which I've put in appendix B for those of you who want to know more about where we get our fossil fuels. In this section I briefly explore the path we're on, and some of the relevant issues involved in developing and adopting alternatives. If you aren't interested in this right now, skip over this section and move on, knowing the information is here as a reference if you want it.

One hundred and thirty thousand miners (give or take a few) would be out of a job if we stopped burning coal. However, some very good news is that jobs created by introducing renewable energy sources more than compensate for jobs lost. Pursuing alternative energy sources requires a workforce that can set up wind turbines, install solar panels and run biomass plants. In 2006, 8.5 million "green-collar jobs" were created, and in 2007 Congress passed and President Bush signed the Green Jobs Act, part of the Energy Independence and Security Act, to train workers for green-collar jobs. Veterans, displaced workers (like coal miners), at-risk youth and families in poverty were targeted for the training. Within a few weeks of being inaugurated, President Obama committed to creating 2.5 million jobs in the first two years of his administration as part of the stimulus plan, many of which would be green energy jobs. Pursuing alternative energy sources does require coal miners to retool and learn how to put up wind turbines, but it does not mean people will be out of work.

Other countries are phasing out coal-fired power plants. Germany has cut its coal use by 37 percent since 1990, replacing coal-based electricity with wind-generated electricity, and the United Kingdom by 43 percent, replacing it with North Sea natural gas. In the United States there is mounting opposition from individuals, towns and states to stop the building or expanding of coal-fired power plants, and since 2002 plans for one hundred new coal plants have been cancelled. California, Washington, Florida, Minnesota, Texas and Kansas no longer allow electric companies to establish new contracts to import electricity from coal, or to construct new coal-fired power plants in their states.

In 2007 the Oregon legislature passed the Oregon Renewable Energy Act, requiring utilities to develop new, homegrown (local) renewable sources. At least 25 percent of Oregon's electricity is to come from wind, geothermal, biomass and solar energy by 2025. Since 43 percent of Oregon's electricity already comes from hydropower, it is a state on its way toward helping individuals, companies and communities light, heat and run on renewable energy. Renewable energy is free and squeaky clean, but the structures needed to capture that energy are not free and can negatively impact other ecosystems.

*Hydropower.* People have harnessed moving water to grind grain, press oil and pump water for centuries. Hydropower is one of two primary renewable energy sources used around the world. Energy comes from running water through turbines as it flows downstream. We use major rivers to power cities, like the Columbia and Colorado Rivers in the United States, but even running water through small channels can power individual homes or industries. Seven percent of our nation's energy comes from hydropower, and nearly a quarter of our world's energy is generated by water. Expanding existing dams can increase energy from hydropower. Building more dams is another possibility. But dams cause other problems, so new dams are scrutinized carefully for their disruption to the flora, fauna and creatures living along the river, and the fish that return upstream to spawn. Constructing fish ladders to help salmon negotiate the dams and placing dams where the disruption to the local habitat is less significant are ways to minimize these negative impacts. On the plus side, new dams create new wildlife habitats and are one of the least expensive ways to expand green energy.

*Biomass.* The second most significant source of green energy is biomass. When we build a campfire and roast hot dogs and marshmallows we are using biomass to warm and cheer us, and to cook our food. Historically, most biomass use has involved burning wood; but most significantly, a good chunk of this free source of energy can be harnessed from our garbage. Residues of agricultural crops, wood waste, the "black liquor" waste from making paper and pulp, and the methane gas from landfills, livestock, municipal solid waste and municipal water treatment plants can all be converted to biopower. Biomass is becoming part of our waste management—taking stuff that would sit in landfills and recycling the energy from it.

Currently most of the biomass produced for energy is used in industry. Paper mills use their own residues (and that of their communities) to fuel the paper-making process, encouraging residents to drop off lumber scraps and woody yard debris for them to convert to energy to run the mill. Besides biomass energy used in boilers, furnaces and stoves, some is being used to fuel cars, trucks and boats that use liquid fuels (such as ethanol or biodiesel) that come from plants. When biomass comes from crops grown for fuel, rather than from recycling waste products into energy, it becomes controversial. Factory farming of biomass crops (planting acres of land with corn) has all the problems of monocultural farming, but the greatest concern is using agricultural land to produce corn for burning when we are in the midst of a global food shortage.

*Geothermal.* Geothermal systems generate power from the earth's warmth. Wells are drilled in the ground and pipes are placed deep into the earth where water (or other fluids) collect the heat and bring it to the surface. Three types of systems provide varying amounts of geothermal energy to users. At the low end are geothermal pumps that heat and cool individual homes, in the middle are direct-use systems that provide power for industrial uses, and the highest producing systems are deep reservoirs that convert thermal heat into green electricity for states to distribute to individual homes, businesses and public services. States in the west have higher subterranean temperatures and are the best places for geothermal systems. California, Hawaii, Nevada and Utah provide some of their state's energy with geothermal power. The most significant drawback to geothermal systems is the start-up expense.

*Wind.* Like water, wind has been used for centuries to generate power—primarily to pump water and grind grain. Wind farms have been set up in thirty-two states, particularly in places where higher winds blow. While only about 1 percent of our energy currently comes from wind, it is an expanding green energy source, and the American Wind Energy Association has released a plan to boost that output to 20 percent by 2030. Individuals in rural or semi-rural areas can install wind turbines and produce their own electricity, although a downside of wind turbines is their high start-up expense. However, currently state and federal tax incentives make it more affordable. Older models were noisy; newer models now make about the same noise as a washing machine. While some birds fly into the blades, fewer fly into the blades than into other buildings we've erected across the landscape—including our homes.

*Solar.* When Mark and I were in Greece in 2008 leading a Juniors Abroad trip for George Fox University, we noticed how many homes had hot-water tanks attached to their rooftops. I learned later that these flat plate collectors absorb heat into water and provide hot water for homes. Solar heat comes in one of two ways. One is passive—heat from the sun coming through windows to light and heat a room. The other is through photovoltaic cells placed (generally) on rooftops that convert sunlight directly to electricity. This free energy accounts for about 1 percent of our current energy use in the United States. Although it is free and clean, it costs a fair bit to install, and discarded collectors, panels and storage devices make it less "green" than systems that don't wear out or need replacing. As with wind, the electricity generated is dependent on external factors—most importantly, how much exposure do the panels get to the sun? Energy collected during the daylight cannot be stored for later use. But residential units can be connected to the local electricity grid and people can sell their extra when they have it. When combined with other green sources, solar becomes an important partner in producing clean and sustainable energy for our homes and industries.

### WHY, THEN, SO LITTLE USE OF GREEN ENERGY?

Even though we have all these options, we don't use more renewable energy for several reasons. First, renewable energy sources are expensive to set up—both for individuals who might put up solar panels, and for businesses and schools, electric companies and cities, who know that while the energy is free, harnessing it, turning it into electricity and transporting it are not.

Second, location, location, location! The best place for setting up wind turbines is Alaska. Unfortunately Alaska is a tad bit remote from the rest of us. Building transmission lines to get the energy into metropolitan areas from rural ones is expensive. But we've built pipelines for gas and oil (most significantly, perhaps, the Trans-Alaska Pipeline completed in 1977 that pipes oil to a port where it can be shipped to the lower forty-eight states), and we continue to plan and build pipes for natural gas, so conversations about getting energy from one place to another have precedent. Change on this scope takes political will—like it did when Eisenhower approved the Highway Act that resulted in roads being built across the nation to make it easier to transport ourselves, merchandise and food across the country.

A third reason we don't use more renewable energy is because solar panels and windmills and biomass sound wacky. Although we Westerners embrace a good share of wacky innovations, we embrace innovations rather selectively; I'm thinking, at the moment, of phones people attach to their ears as they walk around in public. We embraced cell phone plans without much pause, even the ones we don't attach to our ears. But then, cell phones give us immediate benefit. We have a more difficult time embracing an expensive technology that we haven't been convinced we need. Maybe cell phone marketers are just better at convincing us we need the latest communication device than the alternative energy folks are at convincing us we need green energy. But I imagine we buy cell phones because we can see the immediate advantage of them, and because, well, everyone else has one. Maybe that's what we need: a groundswell of people willing to pay more for energy to make it sustainable—and for that groundswell to become somehow visible. We need help to see a bigger picture that benefits me less than it benefits my children and my grandchildren. It is an investment in the future—but not necessarily my future. Perhaps that fact makes it most difficult of all.

A bird just flew into my house. I cringe when that happens. This tragedy, however small in the big scope of things, reminds me that my comforts and conveniences impact God's creatures with whom I share this space. And if I let myself see it, I also know my choices impact the lives of God's people living with me around the world. The most difficult challenge is to keep the big picture in front of us without feeling paralyzed, and to let it move us to useful intentional action. The best way to do that is to choose to follow one piece of the story—perhaps the fate of the Tuvalu people, or the fate of the Appalachian Mountains and their inhabitants, or the residents of the Arctic. Learn about them, begin to pray for their well-being; then you will likely find it easier to keep this a relevant issue because you care about people and places that are impacted by your choices. Once you have opened your heart to some other part of the world affected by your choices, doing something about it will have more urgency. Following are simple, direct questions to that end.

- What positive step will you take this week that will cost only some time and perhaps a degree or two of comfort? (For example, defrost your freezer and clean your refrigerator coils, bump the thermostat up or down to decrease energy you use to cool and heat your home.)

- What is another step you can take this week that will require a small investment in time and/or money? (Invest in a clothesline to hang up your laundry, begin to replace your light bulbs with CFL bulbs, sign up for the green energy plan with your electric company.)

- What lifestyle choices can you begin to contemplate? (Take up walking or biking as a mode of transportation around town, start saving for an energy-efficient vehicle, look into state and federal incentive plans for increasing the energy efficiency of your home.)

- What can you do to encourage your community to join the broader conversations around them—either at church or your place of employment, the local school, or other places of civic engagement? (Start a conversation or campaign to change thermostat settings in public buildings or at your church or workplace, and to replace light bulbs.)

We can live well, love life and embrace the goodness of God's creation. If I decide to fill my hot tub five months a year, I want to enjoy the warmth of a night soak, breathing in air studded with stars, or lit by the moon, or darkened by rain clouds ready to nourish the earth. I can relish this choice if I also let myself be uncomfortable enough with the hard questions, educate myself and make choices aligned with my commitment to walk gently and to love others. When you and I do so, we are joining a groundswell of folks around the world who are building a sustainable future for our children's children.

o   o   o

## RESOURCES

*How can I learn more about energy use in my home?*

- Energy Star. Energy Star is a U.S. Environmental Protection Agency and U.S. Department of Energy program aimed at helping us save money and protect the environment through energy-efficient products (primarily appliances) and practices. The website is full of useful information.

  *1200 Pennsylvania Ave NW*
  *Washington, D.C. 20460*
  *Phone: (888) 782-7937*
  *www.energystar.gov*

- The British Broadcasting Corporation (BBC) offers a fun, interactive, what-you-can do site on the Web.
  *www.bbc.co.uk/bloom/flash.shtml*

### Where can I learn more about alternative energy?

- National Atlas launched American Environmental Atlas to make information available to help us understand continental-scale environmental issues. The North American Environmental Atlas is intended for use by both environmental scientists and the citizens of the United States, Canada and Mexico.

  *www.nationalatlas.gov/articles/people/a_energy.html*

- American Wind Energy Association

  *1501 M Street NW, Suite 1000*

  *Washington, D.C. 20005*

  *Phone: (202) 383-2500*

  *www.awea.org*

- Renewable Energy Policy Project

  *1612 K Street, NW, Suite 202*

  *Washington, D.C. 20006*

  *www.repp.org*

### What can I do to make my existing vehicle more fuel-efficient, and if I'm looking at getting a new vehicle, which are the most fuel-efficient or clean?

- Fuel Economy. The website offers information on fuel economy and on how to make your vehicle more efficient, a list of fuel-efficient vehicles to buy, and more.

  *www.fueleconomy.gov*

- Green Vehicle Guide—United States Environmental Protection Agency:

  *www.epa.gov/greenvehicles*

### How can I change small things in my daily life that will be better for the environment?

- 21 Ways to Conserve Energy. Here you'll find practical suggestions to use things we already do to help the environment. This page will link you to many others that show you how to carry out the twenty-one practical suggestions.

*www.practicalenvironmentalist.com/21-practical-ways-to-help-the-environment*

- The Empowerment Institute offers twenty-five years of research and program development for individuals to use in their homes, schools and communities. Training and informational resources are available.

  *www.empowermentinstitute.net/lcd/*

- 100 Ways to Save the Environment. This site offers suggestions for home, the office, the yard, water supplies and trash.

  *www.seql.org/100ways.cfm*

# PRELUDE

## Except for God

*Gye Nyame*

I'm not very savvy when it comes to following daily news. It's embarrassing to admit how often in the last six years someone has brought up some large world event that I've been clueless about. I do, however, tend to catch hold of a story and become engrossed in it for a number of days. Such was the case in 2009 when I heard about Nadya Suleman, the single mother from California who had octuplets via in vitro fertilization (IVF); already having six young children at home, this made her a mother of fourteen. The public reaction interested me. Loud voices of protest came from all directions regarding an issue that is often treated with silence. Family planning is usually understood to be a private matter not open to discussion. Something must be different about Nadya's case that people felt free to state their opinions with vehemence. Why was the public's response so loud and persistent? Because she is a single mother? Because her children were conceived by IVF?

The extremity of this case broke open a conversation that has been murmuring under the surface. How do we balance what has traditionally been treated privately but increasingly has public consequences? Nadya's story teaches us that we live in a day where family planning is no longer treated solely as a private issue. Maybe the story of Nadya's family captured our attention because it served as a safe place to talk about what traditionally has been taboo. Should we have policies around a woman's choice to give birth to lots of children? Especially, perhaps, if her choice is going to cost the rest of us something because her offspring will consume more than her "share" of our nation's economic and natural resources?

Nadya became an exaggerated caricature, which is much easier to criticize than a neighbor who has three kids and is pregnant with her fourth. She also became a scapegoat of sorts, with the public outcry reflecting our need and desire to have places to discuss our conflicted feelings about this topic. I am also conflicted. While I admire the high value of life Nadya holds in desiring to bring to life all of the embryos her first IVF procedure created, at the same time I worry for the welfare of these children—the complications that come with being born prematurely, and the financial and emotional stress of having fourteen children and only one parent. I also find myself conflicted over the expensive technology we use to create life, especially when there are already so many lives on this planet that could benefit from having a place and a family to call home.

My conflicted response to Nadya's story reflects the complexities of these issues. On one hand I am quite delighted that my parents continued to have children after Rae, and even decided to have one more after Sarah (I am the youngest of three girls). And at the other end of the spectrum I understand the need for women to birth fewer children for the sake of the world. As my husband, Luke, and I contemplate what this will look like for us we imagine having two biological children and adopting a few others.

While at the Crisis Nursery Center in Lilongwe, Malawi, I had an overwhelming desire to create a home for the children there. The Crisis Nursery Center brings in abandoned or malnourished children; about half of the babies will go back to their families in the village when they are renourished and the others hopefully will find a home. I looked upon beautiful and unclaimed faces, and desire, passion and love for the infants compelled me to plan on building my family through adoption. For almost five years now I have talked openly about this desire to adopt, even trying to figure out how I might adopt and finish college at the same time (with the help of my rational, pragmatic father I quickly discovered this was inconceivable, and for good reason). Yet now that I am at a place where I can think about adoption, I am bombarded by the realities that this entails: the complications of international adoption, the financial requirements that accompany adoption and the fear of being an inadequate crosscultural mother. As I stop daydreaming and step out into reality with all of its messiness and logistics I realize what a complex issue family planning really is, and have gained a new respect for couples who have built their families this way.

The *Gye Nyame* is perhaps the most popular of the Akan symbols, translated "Except for God," referring to God's supremacy and omnipotence. The symbol goes along with the proverb *"Abode santan yi firi tete; obi nte ase a onim n'ahyase, na obi ntena ase nkosi n'awie, Gye Nyame,"* translated "This great panorama of creation dates back to time immemorial, no one lives who saw its beginning and no one will live to see its end." This is a comforting symbol of God's omnipotence. Nothing can happen, fortune and misfortune, except by the will of God.

Sometimes when teaching or preaching I ask a leading question that will provide an anticipated response which then becomes my jumping-off place for the next point I'm about to make. I tried doing this while helping out with a pastors' workshop in Malawi. It didn't go as planned. I asked what they would do to prepare if they were told their house would burn down tomorrow. I didn't expect them to say, "Nothing, because if you told us that, it means this is the will of God and so nothing we do can stop this." Whatever point I was trying to make plummeted. Nothing? I had supposed they would respond to my question the way I would. With my Western values of efficiency and productivity alongside the urgent need to have a plan and also a back-up plan, I'd have a plan in place to take out my valuables and fight the fire as best I could. But without the response I was anticipating, I could not make my point.

African Christianity is characterized by an incredible amount of faith and trust in God. In Malawi I learned what it means to stand in awe of God. There is something beautiful about submitting one's life to God's will, a humble recognition that God is in the heavens and we are on earth. As beautiful as this is, though, at times it can lead to a sort of fatalism. When we think the will of God is fixed and set and nothing we do will change the outcome of God's will, it can take away a sense of urgency and immediacy. Some variation of fatalism is common in most world religions, and Western Christians have it as well.

Discerning the line between acknowledging and accepting God's sovereignty and becoming fatalistic challenges us all. Yes, God is sovereign, but we still have choices within the bounds of the free will that God has given us. This delicate balance between God's sovereignty and human agency often becomes fused in conversations about children. The conversation becomes stalemated once we refer to God's sovereignty in the situation, for example, "God will give me the number of children that God intends me to have." In a way this is our fatalism.

Similar to family planning, questions surrounding the use of life support and being open to death are complex. During my senior year of high school my close friend David was diagnosed with a brain tumor. I wanted the medical community to do *everything* they could to save his life. Alongside traditional medicine, his parents tried alternative and experimental medical methods; everyone fought with a vengeance to keep him alive. I remember the panic of going into the terminal wing of the hospital to visit him. It seemed there ought to be a way out, that if we just finagled enough we could trick and postpone death.

When it became evident that recovery was not in sight, we all had to shift our mindset from curing to letting go. And David was the one who helped us learn to be open to death. A few weeks before David died, his father called, telling me that David wanted me to give his eulogy at his memorial service. David planned his funeral, from the suit he would wear to the pizza party following the memorial service to "celebrate." He didn't want anyone wearing black. David had an optimistic outlook; he wanted his funeral to be a celebration of his life and a celebration of the new life he was embarking on. When I got off the phone with David's dad, I wept, finally coming to terms with *Gye Nyame*. David knew it was time to let go, and this was the indicator for me too that recovery was not in sight; it was time to gear up for a different sort of journey—one of mourning and loss. David wanted to return home rather than die in the terminal wing of the hospital. Maybe he would have lived a few more hours, days or weeks in the hospital, but he chose to come home, to let go of life surrounded by those he loved and who loved him.

There are no easy answers to the issues around birth control, family planning, life support and death, but we do well to draw from the wisdom of our African brothers and sisters in thinking through the complexities. In Africa, *Gye Nyame,* or "Except for God," extends through the spectrum of life: in the same way that life is welcomed and represents God's will, so too death occurs and is recognized as the will of God. In the United States we say God will provide me with as many children as God wants, yet we fight with all we can to beat off death. We invest millions of dollars in technology to create life and we invest millions of dollars in technology to delay death. It's true, I wish the medical community could have helped David beat his cancer, but if I want the medical community to use our God-given agency to push back death, then for the sake of balance in the world, I need to also embrace my God-given agency to limit the number of children I will birth. Can we choose to rest on God's sovereignty in providing us with as many children as God wants and then attempt to play God in determining how numbered our days are? I'm not suggesting encouraging particular legislation regarding population control, but rather I'm challenging the church to be more thoughtful in our theology around these complex matters, so that we might be more consistent throughout the spectrum of life and death.

God has provided humans with agency. Agency can be utilized in deciding your family size, and agency can be used in fighting for your life or in letting go of life. The fact that we have agency makes this issue complex. We shouldn't wait for news stories such as Nadya to talk about population, because these conversations often occur in exaggerated and heated forms. We need to have more thoughtful, gentle, honest conversations on how to approach the population crisis.

# SUSTAINING THE BLESSING OF FAMILIES

*But the young ones in the nest—they had been the little*
*warm green spot in the wilderness—the inmost, sweetest joy of his life.*

—LAVRANS, THINKING OF HIS CHILDREN IN
*KRISTIN LAVRANSDATTER* BY SIGRID UNDSET

In the dark night of an early morning during high school, I witnessed our family dog, Jem, give birth to two little puppies. Her calmness amazed me. She was a first timer, yet seemed okay with it all and knew what to do without my help. Ever since witnessing Jem's participation in the miracle that keeps life moving forward, I've been enchanted by the wonder of pregnancy, birth and parenting. Nursing school was to be the first step toward midwifery, but I never got that far. Eventually I moved on from home health nursing to sociology and teaching college students. A colleague told me I became a midwife of a different sort—working with students as they birth their sense of who and what they are becoming.

Mark said it was poetic that at the point in time when our own

daughters contemplated having children, I pursued doula training. Women helping women. I am coming full circle back to a
dream I've held for many years—to sit with women as they birth
their babies, and to walk alongside them in the first months of
their journeys.

I eagerly anticipate grandchildren and want to be an active part
of their lives. I want to help them plant their own vegetable patch
in our garden, bake bread, build a tree house on Fern Creek, hike
forest and mountain trails. I don't like thinking about a conversation that suggests people should limit how many children they
have (yes, this is *that* conversation!) in light of my own children
limiting the number of children *they* have. My writing buddy, Pam
Lau, asked, "Are you sure you want to go there?" No, I don't particularly *want* to go here, but understanding what it means in the
twenty-first century to be open to life requires us to face that uncomfortable conversation.

Embracing life, and pushing toward the flourishing of life being lived on earth, involves moving beyond a focus on me and my
children and grandchildren. Being open to life means I want to
celebrate *other* people's lives too. And part of celebrating others
and helping them flourish is considering the choice to have no
children, or to have one or maybe two so that other children might
have sustainable lives. I hope this sacrifice of limiting the number
of children we bear will only be required for a relatively short time
of human history; right now, it's something we need to consider to
walk gently. This chapter is that hard conversation.

## WHY PEOPLE LOVE BABIES

A lot of us get gushy around babies, whether humans, puppies,
goats or horses. Their disproportionate bodies and helpless inno-
cence incline us toward empathy and protection—which is a good
thing. If we didn't find them so charmingly disarming we might
soon grow weary of their constant cries for attention and need for

care. Like Dr. Seuss's Mayzie the lazy bird we might be inclined to take a long vacation from parenting until the hard work was done.

Since human babies take a particularly long time to be independent it's especially good that they stay cute for so long; by the time they aren't cute anymore we've become attached enough to figure we might as well finish the job of raising them. This love and attraction we feel toward new life seems about as fundamental to our biological need for survival as our biological drive for sex.

A complete conversation about striving to see and care for creation as God does includes talking about babies—our desire for them, our love of them and how many we're collectively birthing every minute of every day. Yet to take something as sacred and precious as children and make them part of a conversation about creation care is, as I've already named, *uncomfortable*. The belief that children are a blessing of God runs deep in our bones, and to talk of them in the same conversation as recycling plastic feels a fair bit sacrilegious. So let me back off that point a moment and offer a brief history of human population growth, an update on where we are now and a report on where we are projected to be in another forty years.

## A HISTORY OF BABY MAKING

For most of human history our population was fairly low and stable. Estimates put the world population between 150 and 300 million around the time that Jesus arrived as a baby in Bethlehem. It took well over a thousand years for that to double, which it did in about 1350. To put that in perspective, best-guess estimates put the whole world's population during the Middle Ages near the population of the United States now. Women had lots of children, but they didn't all make it to adulthood, and enough other troubles, such as war, famine and disease, kept the overall life expectancy relatively low. People could be wide open to life and birth lots of babies because they were so openly exposed to death.

My neighbors and I didn't worry about our young children con-
tracting smallpox or dying from pneumonia. Penicillin treats in-
fections that used to kill people, high blood pressure can be treated
with medications, and surgery combats an assortment of illnesses
and can repair life-threatening injuries. We are decidedly *not* open
to death, and stop it, or slow its coming, wherever possible.

Besides all that, we can now feed people more efficiently and
predictably. So I don't worry about going to the grocery store and
facing empty shelves. Drought, pestilence and disease that used to
wipe out crops and herds don't rank high on my worry list either.
The Global North still has a pretty secure food supply, and we
can't imagine the alternative, although it is an alternative that
some of our neighbors in the Global South take to bed with them
every night.

The industrial revolution brought stabilizing forces in food production and medical advances, so for a while, birth rates stayed
high while death rates dropped, and populations exploded. The
world reached its first billion people around 1800. And while it
took over 1000 years for it to double from 150 million to 300 million, it only took 125 years to double from 1 billion to 2 billion. It
doubled again, to 4 billion, in less than 50 years (in 1974). In 2026
we expect that to double again. Even with the stringent population control policies of China (which are being relaxed somewhat
as of 2009), and more subtle efforts to control population in other
parts of the world, population models suggest the earth may be
host to 9.5 billion people by 2050.

Imagine a map of the world—a white piece of paper with
pencil-drawn outlines of earth's continents. A pencil dot goes on
the map for each million people. In A.D. 1 about 150 dots darkened
the map, most of them clustered in a few parts of Asia, North Africa and the Middle East. The map is mostly white. Dots are added
as the population grows, depicting how many people are alive at
any given point. So now imagine the map in 2010. It has another

6,650 dots on it—for a total of 6,800. The map is mostly black, with a few small white spaces in the areas of land nearest the North and South Poles.

Thinking of all those dots reminds me of a fruit fly experiment we did in high school biology. We were to map population growth starting with two tiny fruit flies in a large glass aquarium. We gave them a huge food supply (but not an infinite one), and it still ended badly for the fruit flies. But we're talking about people here. People are smarter than fruit flies, capable of making more choices than fruit flies, and can manipulate more resources to their advantage. We can let that fruit fly experiment be what it was and not extrapolate overly much.

So, in summary, our human population explosion began around 1800, mostly through advances in agriculture and medicine that were ushered in with the industrial revolution. The good news is that once people figured out their children were not going to starve or die of disease before adulthood, they started having fewer of them. As a country's death rates declined, eventually, so did birth rates. We saw that happen in the United States, even among specific religious groups, like Mormons, who encourage their members to have large families. Mormons still tend to have larger families than other Americans, but they, too, are on a downward trend and have fewer children than they did fifty years ago.

## ECONOMIC SHIFTS AND FAMILY SIZE

In modern cultures children are expensive. In premodern eras children helped the family economically by working alongside their parents. Back then parents weren't sending children off to soccer camp and college either. Economic realities motivate parents today to have fewer children.

As family farms buckled under the competition of agribusiness, farming families moved to the city. While on the farm children had helped with harvests and animal husbandry; in the bustling city they became a mouth to feed and a body to shelter and clothe. Before child labor laws, children from the lower and lower-middle classes worked in factories and continued to contribute to the family income. But now we send children to school for somewhere between twelve and twenty years to get educated. When middle-class adolescents earn money from babysitting, mowing lawns or a part-time job, they aren't expected to contribute it to the family budget. We don't expect them to care for us in our old age either. Children are decidedly no longer an economic asset to their parents.

Instead of sending children into the field to work we send them to basketball camp, take them to piano lessons and to Chuck E. Cheese's, and plan summer vacations so we can spend some quality time together. And unless you're camping, vacations aren't cheap either. A basic three-day pass at Disney is $229 per child, and $262 per adult. And that doesn't count transporting the family there, hotels, meals, snacks and those mementos that seem to make so much sense at the time of purchase, and so little sense six hours later. Most of us middle-class folks will send our children away to college, and pay some chunk of that endeavor as well. And if you plan to help your children with wedding costs, you aren't yet done dipping into (or emptying out) your bank account. If you believe the websites, which all want you to spend scads of money, the average wedding today costs between twenty and thirty thousand dollars. I have personally seen that it can be done for much less. But the point remains: it is rather expensive to raise children in economies that are not directly tied to the land, which has motivated most folks to have fewer of them.

My mother's family followed the typical population shift for industrializing countries. She was the last of seven children, born on the family farm in Colorado in the early 1930s. She, and each of her siblings, had three or four children, averaging 3.1 per family. My generation (with the exception of a cousin who, along with his wife, believed that God would give them the children God wanted them to have—which ended up being thirteen) all had one to five children. Since four cousins had no children, even with my prolific cousin's large family, our extended family average was 2.8 (without the one cousin it would be 2.3, closer to the national average of 2.1). I come from a particularly pronatal family who values large families. Even so, my extended family has followed the national trend to decrease family size over the course of three generations.

As social norms for family size shift we collectively reinforce the new norms without consciously trying to do so. We label couples as selfish who don't want any children, showing our pronatal proclivities, and stigmatize parents of large families for being out of touch with culture and unaware of the financial burden large families place on the family budget and on community resources. Both couples (and children from the latter couple) experience some social embarrassment for their family size.

So what's the problem? If couples are generally having smaller families, won't we be okay shortly? We may be okay eventually, but not anytime soon. The issue is twofold; the first is related to *continuing growth*, and the second to the *level of affluence* in our lifestyles.

*Continuing growth.* Before the birth rate dropped in industrialized countries, the human population exploded. And while the *rate* of growth is slowing worldwide, our population continues to grow because we are all living longer—the mortality rate, or death rate, has also decreased. If Mark and I had one child, and that child and spouse had only one child, and our grandchild just had one, then we would be working toward decreasing the population, but not without complication. If we had two children, and each of our children had two, then the population would just be replaced, and would eventually stabilize. But remember, I am one of twenty-one grandchildren on one side, and one of fourteen grandchildren on the other side; so even if Mark and I (and all my cousins) only had two children, there would still be (and are) a lot of grandchildren and great-grandchildren living in the John and Anna clan on one side, and the Warren and Verna clan on the other. That's why even if all women from this point forward just have two children, we will still experience overall population growth for a while. China provides an interesting case study.

One billion and three hundred thousand million people live in China; that's 20 percent of all of us. In 1979, with a population nearing one billion, the Chinese government decided China had to control population growth to be able to support and sustain their people. The government implemented a one-child family policy, particularly aimed at controlling population in the cities. With a fertility rate of 1.7, China's population still grew by another three hundred million (about the size of the United States) in the following thirty years. In 2030, China's population policy will come into its full effect, and the population is expected to peak and then begin to drop—except that, as I mentioned earlier, China has just relaxed it's one-child policy due to the complications of having an aging population falling on the shoulders of too few able-bodied, tax-paying citizens. At any rate, by 2030 India, with a fertility rate of 2.8, will be the most populated country in the world at 1.5 billion.

Some demographers and watchers-of-the-world-population say that disease, famine, drought and wars over increasingly scarce resources (like oil, food and water) will check the population— and bring it back into balance. This was the argument of political economist Thomas Malthus in 1800. Malthus said that if we didn't control the population ourselves, outside forces would do it for us, and in rather undesirable ways, resulting in something like the fruit fly experiment. The doomsday he predicted didn't happen, largely because of unexpected advances in agriculture, but neo-Malthusians today say we still ought to heed his warning. We have been fruitful and multiplied. Human population is taxing earth's ability to feed and nurture life at a level that allows for the flourishing of all life. The loving and compassionate choice may be to curb our love for our own offspring so that we can also love the offspring of others—both people and creatures. We do this not only for the sake of others but also for the well-being of our own children and grandchildren.

*Level of affluence.* The second part of the problem is less about the number of people on earth and more about how much fat of the land people are consuming. How many people earth can sustain is an important question, but not the only or perhaps even the most important question. The more relevant question is, at what level, or standard of living? If children born in the United States use twice as many resources as children born in Germany, and 117 times as many as children born in Bangladesh, then perhaps, for a season anyway, we shouldn't have as many children if we want earth's resources to be available to everyone. We have come to realize that the wants and needs as defined by a consumer lifestyle crowd out the ability for others to flourish. Eventually, and perhaps sooner than we imagine, we will feel the impact of our lifestyle more here at home too.

## BUT . . . CHILDREN *ARE* A BLESSING

Yes, even after the poopy diapers, spring evenings sitting on metal bleachers wrapped in blankets watching our youngsters play T-ball, parent-teacher conferences and adolescent temper tantrums—most of us still conclude that children are a blessing. Our love for them is inexplicable, as is how parenting deepens our understanding of God's love of us. Parenting is a tangible marker of our place in the long chain of humanity and, if nothing else, a reminder that our survival as a species depends on a lot of us choosing to love and nurture a couple of the creatures into adulthood.

Most nations are pronatal. After all, the surest way to build a population that will accept the norms, values and traditions of a group is to birth them. (Incidentally, this holds true for most religions as well.) Even if a nation is trying to limit population growth, it will still seek to protect and nurture its children. We can't help ourselves. Birthing babies is a biological drive and a social survival strategy. Some nations give tax incentives for having children, and tax breaks for raising them. We pool our resources to teach them to read, write and do arithmetic. We collectively do a pretty good job of getting them vaccinated and fed. Care of a nation's young is a sign of health, morality and goodness. So our inclination is to disregard someone suggesting people should limit the number of children we have; they are Scrooge-like souls immune to the miracle and goodness of new life. Perhaps more significantly, though, having someone tell us we ought to have fewer children challenges our right to have as many children as we want, or as God gives us.

But what if we had to answer to the global community more directly for our choices? What if we could see the cost to mothers, fathers and children of fighting over control for oil in their homeland—oil that is used to bring food to my family table and clothes for my children? What if I could watch the suffering in Honduras and other banana-producing countries at the hands of mercenaries hired by Dole and Chiquita who use violence against farmers and families to maintain absolute control of the banana industry? Or, more positively, what if I could witness the link between a choice for my family to primarily eat a plant-based diet and the grain that becomes available and affordable for children in Ghana? What if all these invisible links suddenly became visible? Would I feel empowered by the difference my choices could actually make?

Once we have children the choices we have shift toward those of how lightly, or heavily, we will live. We can model walking gently, celebrating the goodness of creation by living lightly, using no more than our share of earth's resources, perhaps fewer even, to compensate some for our fellow citizens who use more.

When Mark recently explained his choice to eat a mostly plant-based diet, he did so this way: when he is sitting at a table with others, he notes how much food is available, and is careful to not take more than his share as the platters are passed, even if he is particularly hungry. If the meal is meager (seldom the case in most of our households) he may have to choose either the lentil curry or the bread with honey so that everyone at the table can have something. Mark wants to think that way on a global scale too. Just because he *can* take two servings of lentil curry, he wants to be mindful of the invisible six-and-a-half billion drawing sustenance from the same soil, the same oceans, our collective home. This is not our grandmother's conversation about cleaning our plate because of hungry children in India. We aren't going to send our extra lentil curry to Chad, or give it to the thousands of hungry children who go to sleep in the United States every night. But it is about being intentional about what we, and our children, and our children's children will consume, and working to consume no more (perhaps less) than our share of the abundance of goods, like food, timber, water, oil and coal, that we harvest and mine from God's fertile and giving earth.

We live in a time when the world's children could all drink water that will not make them sick, go to bed satisfied and get up in the morning to go to school. The more visible our global community becomes the more connections we will be able to make between our own children's struggles to learn and those of children learning to read, write and do arithmetic in Uganda, Afghanistan and Peru. We can be hopeful of making the world a better place for all children. Our capacity and desire to love, care for and work toward the well-being of children not our own comes from God, who adopted us, and endowed us with the potential for great love. We are not fruit flies. We have more choices.

## SO, WHAT TO DO?

Some of what's being done is related directly and indirectly to public policy—which helps shoulder the responsibility and burden. And some of what's being done has to do with the personal choices that remain ours—our family size, how we think about contraceptives, adoption, and how gently we walk as families.

*The role of public policy.* Although economics explain some of the reason couples in the United States now have fewer children, government policy contributed to that too. We've not had anything so drastic as China's one-child policy, but stabilizing the U.S. population has been a national goal since the early 1970s. In 1969 President Nixon established a population commission to study the issues of growth in the United States, and after studying it for three years, the commission reported in 1972 that there would be no collective benefit to the U.S. from continuing to grow the population. The commission offered a number of recommendations to help stabilize it, and over the next ten years these became part of U.S. policy.

One recommendation was to limit immigration—and we continue to fight for a balance between keeping our doors open to seekers from other lands, and closing our doors against the same. Another was to ratify the Equal Rights Amendment (ERA), which would make it easier for women to gain access into careers they would find satisfying. The ERA was never ratified—it felt too radical at the time—but doors opened anyway for women, who are now more likely to go to college and establish careers than they were prior to the 1970s. The commission's recommendation was based on the observation that girls who go to college are more likely to postpone marriage and childbearing. The longer women postpone those, the fewer children they have. The more meaningful women find work, the more likely they are to fit children (and fewer of them) around it.

Another set of recommendations was related to conceiving babies. They included making contraceptives more available to women, including to minors, removing restrictions on those who desired voluntary sterilization, and supporting the legalization of abortion.

The upshot of economic factors that inclined us to have fewer children, and policy recommendations that encouraged the same, is that the fertility rate in the United States decreased, waffling between 1.8 and 2.1 for the last couple of decades. But this transition didn't slide into place smoothly; it has been borne out of deeply felt controversy. The commission's recommendations raised a number of ethical issues, and our differing values have kept this conversation lively as we strive for the best ways to stabilize our population while honoring our history as a country that welcomes seekers, respects personal choice and protects life. I believe in the sanctity of life and am pro-life; I want to see this conversation unfold in ways that protect the unborn and provide well for children already born.

*The role of personal choice.* Bill McKibben, an ecologist and a Christian, urges readers from the United States to think about the human population explosion in personal ways in his book *Maybe One: A Case for Smaller Families.* We tend to think of population control in the abstract, or globally, putting the burden on countries where the population explosion is greatest. After all, we say, they are the ones in the most trouble; shouldn't *they* be the ones to stop having babies? But global population is a personal matter particularly because of all those invisible links: Americans use a lot of the globe's stuff, even simple renewable stuff, like water.

In my Sociology of Religion class we talked about the role of religion in controlling, directing and advising people regarding sexuality, and eventually talked about contraceptives. A number of us still harbor ambivalence about the role of contraceptives when we think about what it means that God blesses people with children. Should the number of children we have be our choice? Just because we can control fertility, should we?

QuiverFull is a movement among conservative Christians that encourages couples to see children as God's blessing and seeks to support large families. Online blogs, resources and literature connect families that may otherwise feel isolated in their choice to have large families. A lot of you became familiar with the movement through Jim Bob and Michelle Duggar, who allow cameras to follow their clan on the TLC reality TV show *19 Kids and Counting.* The Duggars have become a conversation centerpiece for both those in favor of and those critical of the QuiverFull movement.

The Catholic Church's position on contraception affirms life and being open to life, and in some ways, QuiverFull is a Protestant affirmation of the Catholic position. Sex is about more than procreation, says the Catholic Church; it is also about pleasure, and emotional bonding, but procreation should not be separated from sex. In *The Theology of the Body,* Pope John Paul II reaffirmed the Catholic Church's convictions. To separate sex from procreation increases the likelihood that women will be seen by men as objects for sexual pleasure, increases pressure for women to participate in premarital sex, and focuses too much on sex *only* for pleasure without the accompanying responsibility that comes from being open to life whenever one is open to sex.

Natural Family Planning is promoted and taught within the Catholic Church as an acceptable way to plan pregnancies. Essentially its message is, if you don't want children, don't have sex when you are fertile. A woman learns to read her body's cues to know when she could get pregnant, and she and her husband choose not to have sex during the three to seven days every month when she is fertile.

In the 1930s Protestant denominations largely embraced the use of contraceptives to control family size, affirming the value and purposes of sex for pleasure and for the emotional bonding that could be separated from the procreative aspects of sex. But Protestants haven't been as thoughtful or as careful about educating women about how contraceptives work, which is perhaps part of what makes QuiverFull an attractive alternative to some couples. Most Protestants don't distinguish much between types of contraceptives, or give much thought to whether those differences are worth thinking about. Barrier methods (for example, condoms) prevent fertilization from occurring. Hormonal contraceptives—which now come in the form of pills, implants, injections and IUDs—don't always prevent ovulation from taking place (sometimes they do and sometimes they don't), but they effectively prevent a fertilized egg from setting up residence in the uterus. That's a problem for some Christians. Besides, hormonal contraceptives fool and manipulate a woman's body and keep it from doing what it was created to do, and the research is still out on the various long-term effects manipulating hormones and menstrual cycles has on women's health. While Protestants didn't want to err on the side of making sex all about procreation, they may have erred on the side of not helping Protestants be adequately thoughtful and informed about contraceptive choices.

I'm drawn to the thoughtfulness of the Catholic perspective. Yet, to love others requires me to limit the impact I will make on the earth—including the impact I make because of the children I birth who will have children of their own. As a species, humans have stayed mostly open to life, though we now use contraceptive technology to control just how open. Closed to death, we use other technology to push back death. We have managed to significantly decrease infant and childhood deaths and to postpone adult death. Yet, without that birth/death balance we have overextended ourselves as a species. We have filled earth with humans, instead of being stewards of earth's potential to be a flourishing home for all God's creation. To pursue what is merciful and just, do we need to think differently about what it now means to be open to life? What it means to foster the flourishing of other people's lives?

This becomes a collective argument—any couple's choice is only one couple, but each individual choice impacts generations to come, contributing to the well-being of others who sit at the table with us today and will join our children and grandchildren at the table tomorrow. Can we be open to life collectively by limiting our own children so that we might make it more possible for other children to flourish?

I've not likely convinced the lot of you that feeding, growing and nurturing a third, fourth or fifth child means a houseful of children in Africa or Southeast Asia go hungry. The connections are complex, and the links come through a thousand different hands. Our biggest challenge may be to see the world as one connected whole, and our choices as impacting it collectively rather than individually. Yes, the exploding population is currently elsewhere, mostly in the Global South, yet families in the Global North use far more of earth's resources to grow our families.

Some parents who want large families but feel compelled to limit how many children they birth enlarge their families through adoption. Adoption provides homes for children, and children for homes, with extra room to go around. Those who open their homes to love the child of another demonstrate something of our own adoption as children into the family of God. Adoption is a picture of love extended, reinforcing that the world is one large family where, beneath our disagreements about politics, religion and values, we have something in common: reproducing the next generation. We remember our goodness as a people when we open our hearts to children who are not our biological offspring. Adoption is one way to love the world's children one child at a time.

Nothing is without its critics, controversy and complication, however, and that includes adoption. For one, we adopt selectively; race matters when it comes to children we adopt. According to a Christian adoption counselor the hierarchy in the United States goes something like this: white babies find homes most easily, followed by biracial Latino/white babies, then Latino or Asian babies, followed by African American girl babies, and then Down syndrome babies, and finally African American boy babies. Older children in the foster care system are least likely to be adopted. While white couples preferring white infants makes sense (we tend to want children who will look like us), racism and fears of difference based on racial stereotypes also factor into our decisions of what children we adopt and which ones we pass over.

I have great admiration for parents who accept the challenges and complications that accompany interracial and international adoption. Such parents must ask what responsibility they have to the ethnic culture out of which they remove a child to raise in their own. How best do non-Asian adoptive parents teach daughters about their Chinese heritage and context, or African American sons about theirs, especially if parents are raising them in white neighborhoods? Some concerns get raised about whether or not international and interracial adoption can be done well. Other concerns are raised about adopting children from the Global South who would live lightly on earth in their own country and moving them to a country that lives on it heavily. Both present valid questions.

While family size—through adoption or birth—is a significant piece of the conversation, the other significant question besides "how many people can earth sustain?" is "at what level of sustenance?" Some of our heavy living is beyond our control. Unless we work at home, most of us go to school or work in buildings that use heating and air conditioning and keep some security lights on twenty-four hours a day. Most of us will drive to get wherever we're headed for the day's task. Most of us will eat food we have not grown ourselves, nor bought from our neighbors. Most of us will own computers that will be replaced every three or four years, along with a lot of other communication and electronic gadgets. So while having smaller families is one piece of the population puzzle, becoming a family that leaves a light footprint matters most. Regardless of our family size we can all become families that walk lighter. We can bike and walk more to *get* places, not just for recreation, carpool and use public transportation, grow vegetables, shop locally, buy used, and eat lower on the food chain.

We can choose to love the world's children collectively. To live lightly as we strive to see it, and love it all as God can and does. Perhaps being open to life involves embracing, laughing with and growing our children, while also nurturing our neighbors' children—some of whom we will bring into our homes to raise—and children who are born, raised and live south of us, and across the Pacific and Atlantic Oceans.

## WHY IS THIS SO HARD?

I ask my students under what grounds it might be ethical for China to establish a one-child policy. It's a difficult question—some can't see how it could *ever* be ethical. We come from a culture that values individual rights, the freedom to choose our own way. We want people to choose to be good citizens, but we'd rather they be bad citizens than be forced to be good ones. We'll punish folks that step across the line and rob a store or embezzle funds, but we value freedom enough to let people make a lot of choices that primarily serve their own interest, even if those choices hurt themselves, or the greater community. China's ethical principles are less focused on individual rights than on ensuring that the good of everyone is protected. The responsibility to make choices that do not harm the community trumps individual rights to make choices that benefit oneself.

The population challenge is a "tragedy of the commons" problem that reflects this difference between an individual rights focus and a community responsibility focus. If I'm the only farmer that lets my cows graze at will on the pasture I share with my community, there is no problem. But if everyone lets their cows graze at will on the common pasture, the pasture will die and not be able to renew itself and feed any cows. So, should we leave it up to individuals to make the choice to determine how much grazing their cows will do on the pasture, or should the pasture use be regulated? So far we are landing on the side of personal freedom and self-regulation when it comes to reproductive choices. Childbearing is a matter we think of as private and personal, even if it has public and global implications.

I am *not* advocating China's policy. I rather appreciate that we have a constitution that protects us from this level of government interference. In place of government mandates, can we have this conversation in our churches and with our friends and family? It may be more uncomfortable because we are treading in the realm of personal choice, but it will resonate more fully with our perspectives on responsible freedom, justice and compassion. We need help to see the bigger picture. We need a community of others thinking carefully and well about family size.

To limit one's family size requires a willingness to forgo what I want in order to embrace something else for the good of another. This is particularly difficult because those others are mostly invisible to me. Granted, for couples who don't want children the choice is easy, and I appreciate the contribution they make to the solution by not having children. When those of us who want children choose to limit the number we will bring into the world we do it because of love. We are staying open to life and embracing it radically through our sacrifice. We are willing to do so because we love our children—the ones living under our roofs, and the ones living around the world.

May we relish the miracle of life that comes through us by way of children! Give birth to one, or maybe two, and if you want to fill your quiver, adopt children who long for homes and a place to be loved. And in all cases, may we learn to live simply and lightly, to laugh heartily, and with the spaces created by doing more with less, release earth's abundance into the loving of God's other children.

o   o   o

## RESOURCES

### *Further Reading*

McKibben, Bill. *Maybe One: A Case for Small Families.* New York: Plume, 1999. McKibben argues for why families in the United States, high consumers of the world's resources, ought to consider limiting their family size for the sake of us all. He makes it personal, talking about the difficult choice he and his wife made to only have one child.

# PRELUDE

## It Is God Who Swats the Flies for the Tailless Pig

*Aboa a onni dua Onyame na oprane ho*

During my first week in Malawi I went to the grocery store with my host sister Grace Quarter-Sey. I started to recommend my divide-and-conquer strategy for our grocery list but stopped myself, remembering that the Malawian value of relationships and shared experiences was more important than my instinct to be efficient. Grace and I are both products of our different cultures. Mine values efficiency, productivity and progress, and these have helped make our nation strong and wealthy. Grace's culture values relationships, traditional ties and being present to the moment, and these have helped to form rich, meaningful community and a culture that experiences the full spectrum of their humanity. We all live out of our particular culture's values and norms, although we seldom recognize the invisible power our cultural values have in our lives and over our choices until they bump up against some other culture that lives differently.

In this book I've used the preludes to make the invisible visible. Seeing creation as the better starting point for our theology rather than the Fall; understanding that we are already united with others, that our unity is a fact and our strength lies in it; seeing that in taking care of earth we are taking care of each other—all of these are seen more easily through the eyes of peoples whose worldviews have not been shaped by Western ideals. I'm not suggesting the West has it all wrong and the Global South has it all right. They have their own blind spots, like the fatalism that can keep them passive rather than working toward change. But this book has been about *our* blind spots, and what we can learn from others outside our culture.

I first confronted cultural values I took for granted in an anthropology class with Dr. Dean Arnold at Wheaton College. I wondered how much what I believed about Christian ethics had also been shaped by my Western heritage. While at first feeling frightened, I began to explore and challenge some of the taken-for-granted ideas that influenced my daily life, particularly nonreligious values that shaped how I understood and lived out my faith.

I grew up with the idea that the *imago Dei* referred to humans' souls, consciousness and reasoning ability that reflected God's nature and made us distinct from, and superior to, the rest of nature. Dominion became a right, rather than a vocational calling, and a power that belonged to our human nature. Subduing creation was for the sole sake of providing for our human needs. This was the only interpretation of the *imago Dei* I knew. I never questioned it—especially, I suppose, because it validated that I was unique and special and comfortably positioned on top of the totem pole. Unbeknownst to me, this interpretation of the *imago Dei* influenced my actions on a daily basis.

If I no longer believed creation is here to serve my needs, how would my ideas around how to live change?

Many biblical scholars suggest that the *imago Dei* ought to be understood in a different light. When the Hebrew words are read within their context, our likeness to God is less about being conscious, rational creatures and more about filling a social role as we *represent* God on earth through our actions. If we are to represent God, then the dominion we cultivate ought to represent and mimic the way God would rule. God rules the cosmos with compassion, justice and mercy, so we are to cultivate a domain of compassion, justice and mercy.

This understanding of the *imago Dei* flipped the one I had on its head. Creation continues to belong to God, and humans are God's stewards, working toward a peaceful, harmonious creation. Human dominion is to be a benevolent, wise and just rule over earth, so that God's compassion and justice are evident throughout creation.

Every seminarian remembers their first sermon. I most definitely remember mine. It was a hot day in June, and I was preaching at a Presbyterian college in Akropong, Ghana, where over two thousand students sat fanning themselves in the benches and chairs. The sermon was going okay; I actually liked it quite a bit. In the middle of the sermon I popped out of my U.S. English and stammered my way through a Twi proverb I had been practicing all week. The proverb *"Aboa a onni dua Onyame na oprane ho"* means, "It is God who swats the flies for the pig who has no tail." It didn't matter what I said or did after that, the fact that I had used a Twi proverb made the sermon a success. To be honest, it made preaching in Ghana fairly easy; as long as I incorporated Twi proverbs my sermons were pretty much a guaranteed hit.

While I first used proverbs as a tool for contextualizing the gospel, they soon became invaluable assets of my preaching. I began to see how rich and deep these proverbs were, how they de-

scribed a truth so profoundly because they were born out of the
crucible of life. And so in many ways the proverb "It is God who
swats the flies for the tailless pig" is much more powerful than all
the theologizing I can do about the *imago Dei*. It depicts a compassionate God, a God who does not sit high and mighty away from
the day-to-day activities but instead is actively, compassionately
involved in the mundane details, even caring for animals' discom-
fort. God's domain is characterized by compassion and concern.
To be the image bearers of God is to foster this compassionate
concern for the rest of created life. It is God who swats the flies of
the tailless pig. God has compassion even on the swine.

How would we change the way we live if we believe being made
in the *imago Dei* meant that we were God's representatives on
earth? Rather then allowing the bottom line, time efficiency and
cost-benefit analysis to shape our choices, what if at the forefront
we were motivated by love for God's creation, and a desire for justice and mercy? If God's dominion is *shalom* then I would seek
justice for women and children who are overworked and under-
paid in India as they make my clothes. We'd be concerned for how
the cow that provides us with milk and cheese is treated, as well as
the forest creatures and forest from which we extract wood for paper, lumber and fuel. God built principles of shalom into the cov-
enant and Mosaic law, enabling the flourishing of creation. Sabbath laws pertained both to the weekly and yearly cycle. On the
seventh day (and seventh year) the land, animals and laborers were
commanded to rest (Leviticus 25). The command encompassed
and protected the ox, donkey, slaves and aliens (Exodus 23:12).
The sabbath laws and the Year of Jubilee helped to keep society just
and healthy by allowing rest for the animals and servants every
seven days and rest for the fields every seventh year, and by calling
for slaves to be set free and for their land to be returned to their
families every fifty years. If we become serious about reflecting
God's domain perhaps we'll have to wrestle with what sabbath laws

and Years of Jubilee might look like in today's society.

I found three places I could go to look for help in figuring out how to live well and what it looks like to represent God's image to the rest of creation. The first came from a Jewish family. During my last year at Princeton I had the pleasure of being a nanny for the family and gained a deep appreciation of their faith. I was present during many of the Jewish holidays. On *Tu B'Shevat,* or New Year of Trees, they feasted on nuts and other dried fruits in celebration of creation. One of the primary practices for this holiday is to plant trees to show respect and appreciation to the trees and other elements of creation.

I could also draw from my experiences in Africa. Walking around the streets of Lilongwe, Malawi, and Accra, Ghana, I saw signs that read: "God's love hair salon," "God's providence car shop," the "Jesus saves clothing store." To my Western eyes this was all very amusing. I wonder how a "Jesus saves clothing store" would do in the United States? My first thought when I came across these signs was that they represented a strange residue from the nineteenth- and twentieth-century mission project. As I learned about African culture and religion, though, I began to understand where such names came from. For the African there is no separation between secular and sacred; God is intimately interwoven into the fabric of life. Religion is so integrated for Africans that it is not so much an activity as it is tied to their essence as individuals and a society. According to Kenyan theologian John Mbiti:

> Wherever the African is, there is his religion: he carries it to the fields where he is sowing seeds or harvesting a new crop; he takes it with him to the beer party or to attend a funeral ceremony; and if he is educated, he takes religion with him to the examination room at school or in the university; if he is a politician he takes it to the house of parliament.

Living in Africa provided me with an example of what religion in the marketplace might look like, and not just because the names of the shops were religious. Religious names reflect the inescapable nature of a religion that influences all arenas of life.

But perhaps the best example of where I can go for what *imago Dei* looks like is the Israelites in the Old Testament. The Israelites understood that their role as the moral center of creation was to represent God's rule through peace and justice by maintaining and enhancing the quality of life for all creatures. When the Israelites went awry, so did everything under their domain. Throughout the Old Testament we witness the relationship between the obedience of Israel and the fruitfulness of the land. When Israel was in bondage to Egypt or living in disobedience, all aspects of creation suffered.

The prophet Jeremiah speaks most clearly of the adverse effect human sin has on the earth. Because of human wickedness it does not rain (Jeremiah 3:3; 14:4), the land is made desolate (Jeremiah 12:10-13; 23:10; Joel 1:10-20), the animals and birds are swept away (Jeremiah 12:4; Hosea 4:3), and the land is polluted and cries out to God (Jeremiah 3:2, 9; Isaiah 24:4-7; 33:9; Hosea 4:3). The flip side of this is that redemption of the people leads to the redemption of the land. Isaiah describes a picture of a future hope where the wolf and the lamb will feed together, and the lion will eat straw like the ox, where the land and the people are redeemed and live together in peace (Isaiah 65:17-25). The infant will play near the cobra's hole and a young child may put her hand into a viper's nest (Isaiah 11:8). This sounds like a domain characterized by a God who swats the flies for the pig.

In our Western view we tend to see the world through a lens that places humans at the top and in control of an economic, efficient, productive center. We have drifted away from being representatives of God. To be God's representatives will require a shift away from a commodity view of creation to a view of ourselves as moral caretakers.

There are many ways to faithfully devote our lives to Christ, some of which may not naturally seem "religious." What we eat, how we transport ourselves, what clothes we purchase—all these are activities determined by economic factors. God has empowered us as image-bearers to transform religion, to infuse it into the totality of our lives, and to influence our boardrooms, city halls and marketplaces with the values of love, mercy, justice and compassion.

## 8

# FINAL WORDS

*Then God looked over all he had made,*

*and he saw that it was very good!*

—GENESIS 1:31

Adjacent to Fern Creek is an old deserted barn that was used
to dry hazelnuts a lifetime ago. Entering it on a hot summer day
reminds me of walking into the barn on the family farm in Colorado as cool air prickles my skin while my eyes adjust to the dark.
A not unpleasant odor fills the place—some combination of old
wood, burlap bags, hazelnut shells and engine oil. I've explored it
some with Mark, and some on my own, finding glass bottle treasures, old wooden crates and harvesting rakes like we used to help
Mark's parents harvest their hazelnuts years ago. Barn swallows
have taken up residence, and they swoop and fly as we climb the
steps to the upper floors of the barn.

I love visiting the barn, and grieve the day someone will finish
tearing it down (the west wall has already collapsed). I should say,
I *loved* it there. This summer my daughter Rae went over with me,
and as we climbed the stairs she shuddered and said, "Don't the
bats bother you?"

"Bats?" I said. "Aren't those barn swallows?"

She pointed to the rafters and said, "I don't think barn swallows hang upside down."

I have since gone into the barn and tried to *imagine* that the bats swooping over my head were barn swallows. Pretending doesn't work. I'm not someone who is easily disturbed by mice, snakes or slugs, but there is something decidedly disturbing about having rodents with wings flying hither and yon over one's head.

I could make two points here. One is that God made bats too and my response to them is irrational, and likely borne from the tales we heard as children. But I'll skim over that one, and use our nearly universal response to bats to make another point instead.

Once we are confronted with some truth about how the world really is, we can't easily go back to seeing it the way we prefer to see it, the way we saw it before. My only alternative was to not believe Rae and continue to believe the bats were barn swallows. (How I wish I could!) Similarly, I will never see chocolate, eggs or the climate-change conversation the same way I once did. I know something of the story of the children who labor in the cocoa fields, the treatment of chickens in egg-laying factories and the effects of global warming on island countries like Tuvalu. As Rae identified the bats to me, Megan Anna and I have identified those realities to you. That might not have been what you were hoping for from this book, but that is part of what you received.

Perhaps you read this book because you are drawn to conversations about living a life that reflects the good life—a life lived more nearly as God intended. We want that to be simple and beautiful. And much about it is. Living well leads to healthier and happier lives. It shouldn't surprise us that when living well is defined by walking gently it also opens doors for people and creatures around the world to have healthier and happier lives. Living the good life honors God when it is a just and merciful life that moves creation toward *shalom,* that is, the perfection of God's creation, universal flourishing, wholeness, peace.

But conversations about living well can produce more guilt than action. Reading about all the ways to consider walking gently is overwhelming and can be troubling, and I suspect you have had moments of that in the hours you've spent in these pages.

Let me remind you of two things. First, you do not have to completely overhaul your life to make a change that will make a difference. One of the biggest contributions you can make is to raise your voice and join other voices telling our leaders that you want them to do whatever is necessary to bring down our carbon emissions, and to make changes that make us all more responsible stewards of resources. Those changes will cost us all some convenience; we'll pay more for some things, and eventually change some habits, like using disposable bags at grocery stores. Meanwhile, make some changes of your own. You'll likely find that once you make one change others will follow—not because you figure that since you've mastered one (*sigh*), you suppose you should tackle another (*sigh*). Rather, one change will ignite a passion that has you falling in love with this place we call home all over again, perhaps seeing trees and birds the way you did as a child, or seeing them in ways you never have before. Lasting change lasts because it brings joy and satisfaction. Start small. One choice.

Second, like most journeys, walking gently is more satisfying when done with a companion or two. Find a friend to join you in checking out a local farmers' market. Take some children and friends apple or berry picking. See if family members, friends or people from church want to add to your order of fair-trade cocoa or chocolate chips. You'll encourage each other with your commitment to buy fair trade, and save on shipping costs and fuel used to deliver boxes ordered separately. Or think bigger yet and plant your own small community garden, or start one at your church, inviting others to share in the work and the rewards. Or think global and join a global movement.

I was teaching Social Change the fall semester that the International Day of Climate Action organized by 350.org was going to occur and decided the best way to teach a class about social change was to invite them to participate in a social movement. We mobilized George Fox University to action. We divvied up tasks—some made T-shirts with our slogan, "a week of living light," using donated shirts turned inside out, one person created a Facebook site that kept participants connected and informed. Two others talked with publicity folks, including the city mayor, as we planned a march to City Hall to deliver a letter signed by students, faculty and administrators in support of earth-friendly city policies. We had nonvegetarians sign up to eat vegetarian for a day, and got volunteers to form the number 350 on the quad where we took a picture from the rooftop of the science building to send to 350.org, joining thousands of other groups sending photos of their events.

Our class of twelve inspired and helped raise awareness on our campus and in our community, meanwhile letting our local, state and national representatives and international leaders know that we wanted action taken on climate change.

Having people walk alongside you adds accountability and reward. Janet, my walking partner, keeps me faithful. On drizzly days I'd just as soon stay in bed, but I know she is expecting me to show up in the curve of the road between her house and mine, and she knows I'm expecting her to do the same. I've never regretted the choice to get up and go walking.

But walking gently is not always about work. Sometimes it is simply about gathering with friends and pointing each other toward God's goodness.

At our Autumn Equinox party this year we served butternut squash risotto with roasted vegetables, and beet salad from our garden. We made apple cranberry crisp with apples from our little orchard and drank wine from a local vineyard. One person read fall-inspired poetry, another read a children's story, another shared a memory. We saw fall photographs set to music and listened to a side-by-side reading theater. Afterward we meandered down through our toddler forest to the fire pit and sang songs while the fire's light reflected off our faces. We stumbled through Simon and Garfunkel, the Beatles, and a John Denver song or two, eventually settling on more familiar choruses and hymns. We ended what had been a magical night of simplicity, shared friendship, a celebration of changing seasons and God's abundance with "Amazing Grace."

o   o   o

## RESOURCES

*Where can I find resources to use in small group studies or curriculum for Sunday school, or more ideas and actions my family or small group can take?*

- Creation Care, under the Evangelical Environmental Network, offers resources regarding creation care for life, for families and for churches.

  *680 I Street SW*
  *Washington, D.C. 20024*
  *Phone: (202) 903-0209*
  *www.creationcare.org/churches.php*

- Earth Ministry is a non-profit organization dedicated to engaging people of faith in environmental stewardship.

  *6512 23rd Ave. NW, Suite 317*
  *Seattle, WA 98117*
  *Phone: (206) 632-2426*
  *www.earthministry.org/resources*

*What good, informative and interesting videos are available for general education about earth?*

- *Planet Earth* produced by Maureen Lemire. Directed by Alastair

Fothergill. 11 episodes, 60 min. each. British Broadcasting Corporation, 2006. This eleven-part series offers an excellent look at earth, covering mountains, caves, oceans, deserts—everything from pole to pole. It's not overtly political but does push toward conservation of this amazing planet.

# APPENDIX A

# What Might a Home Audit Look Like?

The following numbers offered as my sample audit are based on a national average computed by the Energy Information Administration (EIA) for how much carbon dioxide is emitted per kilowatt hour (kWh). If you want to get precise, you can find out what the kWh is for your state, which depends on the electricity mix in your state—how much comes from coal, natural gas, hydropower, nuclear power, perhaps wind and solar.

Bathrooms. Time your showers. Let's assume you take an eight-minute shower; you can save 342 pounds of carbon dioxide a year by cutting it down to six. Most of us can actually get by *without* a daily shower. No one seems to notice. My mother (a rather godly woman) grew up with a weekly bath—and she shared the bathwater with her siblings since it had to be heated on the stove and brought in from the pump outside. So for starters, time your shower, shorten it, and maybe take the leap and skip a shower now and then. Lowering your water heater from 140 degrees to 120 degrees saves 479 pounds per year, and adding a layer of insulation to your water heater saves more yet.

Bedrooms. Install ceiling fans to lessen your use of air conditioning. Fans use less energy than air conditioning. Think about lighting: how much, how bright and what kind of atmosphere do you want to create? A nineteen-watt CFL light bulb emits about the same light as a seventy-five-watt bulb. (CFL bulbs come in various wattages just like traditional light bulbs.) Assuming you use each light an average of two hours a day, for every traditional light bulb you replace you cut fifty-five pounds a year in carbon dioxide emissions. I counted the lights in our house—we have a ridiculous number of them. (Mark wired our house and has a different propensity for light than I do.) Fortunately most of them seldom get turned on. So, let's say a house has twenty light bulbs (which might be high or low, depending on your house) that get used an average of two hours a day throughout the year. Switching to CFL bulbs would be a savings of 1100 pounds a year. Turning off lights when you leave rooms certainly helps too. If you want to leave a light on, cast a softer light by using a lamp with a low-wattage CFL bulb.

**Kitchen.** Only run your dishwasher when it's full, and use the air-dry option—or better yet, crack your dishwasher to let dishes dry without using electricity. Check out your refrigerator. Can it hold a dollar bill in the door? If the dollar falls out, you're leaking cold air, which means you're also leaking carbon dioxide because you are using more energy to keep things cold. Pull the refrigerator out from the wall twice a year and clean the coils, and defrost your freezer once a year. You can save over seven hundred pounds a year in carbon dioxide emissions by cleaning coils and defrosting your freezer. When you need to replace your refrigerator, or any other appliance, get one rated with the Energy Star label, which means it is energy efficient.

While we're auditing the kitchen, let me mention food again—though ever so briefly. If 30 percent of your daily calories come from meat, dairy and poultry, you emit about 3,274 pounds of carbon dioxide every year. That gets cut in half if you eat a vegetarian diet, and further yet if you eat a vegan diet. But you don't have to go all-out vegan to do the world a bit of good. Just eat lower on the food chain—replace some of the red meat with more fish, eggs or poultry, and experiment with meatless pastas, stews, salads, and rice and bean dishes.

*Garbage.* A lot of towns make recycling easy; in other places you have to work harder at it. Recycling what you can saves a thousand pounds of carbon dioxide emissions a year. Simply recycling what you can and switching light bulbs would decrease carbon dioxide emissions by 5 to 10 percent for the average household in the United States—a significant starting point.

*Laundry.* Ninety percent of the energy used in a washing machine comes from heating the water. Wash in cold water as much as possible, and rinse with cold water. If half the loads you currently wash in hot water were washed in cold water you'd save about seventy pounds a year. The biggest laundry energy user, though, is the dryer. If you dry half of your loads every year and hang the rest up outside (that's about what I manage in our Oregon weather) you'd save 725 pounds of carbon dioxide. If you want to get creative about not using the dryer at all you could hang some drying devices in your home to use during the winter and on rainy days. Put up a clothesline in the basement, or buy a drying rack at Target.

*Living/family room.* Using a power strip for entertainment devices and turning them off when the devices aren't being used saves 240 pounds a year. In the winter, for every degree you set the thermostat below seventy degrees you save 320 pounds of carbon dioxide (assuming you heat with natural gas; if you heat with electricity you save 236 pounds for every degree below seventy). A similar equation works in the summer. For every degree you set the thermostat over seventy-two you save 121 pounds of carbon dioxide. Think about using some of the money you save on electric bills in the next few months to get a programmable thermostat, so you can keep your house comfortable when you're in it, but let it cool down, or warm up, when you're not. Seal areas around doors or windows where cold air is sneaking in during the winter and hot air during the summer.

*Transportation.* Combine errands to keep from making extra trips. Walk or bike when you can. What would it take to figure out a carpool to work? Can you take public transportation? Supporting public transportation is another way to support community efforts to create a sustainable future for your community's children and grandchildren. Buying local food and merchandise not only supports local merchants in your community, it also cuts down on the fossil fuel used to get things delivered to your town or to go get them from some other town.

That's a beginning list—and would be overwhelming if you thought you had to do it all now. Pick one or two ideas to implement as a start. If we all thought about cutting our electricity use by 10 percent a year for five years we'd make a huge dent in our collective energy use and join the global effort to decrease carbon dioxide emissions 50 to 80 percent by 2020.

# APPENDIX B

## A Primer on Traditional Energy Sources

Coal, natural gas and petroleum constitute the primary sources for what we call fossil fuels. Following is some basic information about the different sources—where they come from, how much of them we use, and what is good or problematic about each of them.

*Coal.* Illinois is a large state user of coal. According to the Illinois Office of Coal Development and Marketing, about 50 percent of the state's electricity comes from coal. Illinois is also a fairly large producer of our nation's coal. Twelve counties in Illinois mine it, bringing in nearly a billion dollars of revenue. Coal is the cheapest fossil fuel available to us; it is also the dirtiest, emitting more carbon dioxide than any other fuel source. While we use more petroleum overall than coal, 49 percent of the United State's electricity is generated from burning coal. For comparison, France, a nation that depends heavily on nuclear sources of energy, only gets 4 percent of its electricity from coal. Besides being dirtier, what makes coal worse than oil or natural gas is that 60 percent of the energy that comes from coal is lost just in generating electricity from it and in distributing it.

*Natural gas.* One afternoon when Rae was about four years old and learning to put letters into words, she spelled out G-A-S while we were filling our car with gasoline. When she asked what it was, we told her that we put it in our car to make it run. She said, "So. There are two kinds of gas. The car kind, and the people kind." We smiled and said, "Yes, two kinds of gas." Actually there are more than two, a lot more, but another relevant one for this conversation is natural gas, not to be confused with the car kind or the people kind.

Most of the natural gas burned in the United States comes from the United States. The U.S. produces about 86 percent of what we use, and imports the rest. We use it to heat our homes, to generate electricity, and in the manufacturing of fabrics, plastics, paint, glass and steel. Natural gas burns cleaner and emits fewer harmful byproducts than other fossil fuels; it puts 30 percent fewer greenhouse gases into the atmosphere than oil, and 45 percent fewer than coal. Switching from coal to natural gas is one way Great Britain decreased its overall carbon dioxide emissions.

**Petroleum.** The United States has a fairly good supply of natural gas, and isn't particularly dependent on foreign coal. Much of the fuel needed for electricity in the United States is generated here. But nearly 60 percent of the petroleum that fuels our cars, trucks, airplanes and industry comes from outside U.S. borders—and we use a lot more petroleum than we do coal. One of the agreement points for Republicans, Democrats and Independents is that we are too dependent on foreign oil. We've been importing more oil than we produce since 1993, and politicians agree that dependence on countries like Saudi Arabia for oil compromises our national security.

One way to decrease our dependence on other countries for oil is to pursue drilling in harder-to-access places. We reached peak-oil (the point at which the amount of oil being extracted from oil fields begins to decline) around 1970, but crude oil experts believe that we could drill more untapped resources. One proposal is to drill for this oil while developing sustainable alternatives for energy. These untapped oil pockets are beneath the ocean floor (referred to as "off-shore" drilling) and in protected wilderness areas, like the Arctic National Wildlife Refuge on the northern slope and coast of Alaska.

The other proposal to decrease our dependence on foreign oil focuses energy and money into developing alternative energy sources now—sources that won't contribute to global warming and are sustainable into the future. Proponents claim this focus will boost the economy by developing green-collar jobs, lowering our dependence on foreign oil and providing an immediate response to global warming. This last bit is the assumption and hope of the 2009 stimulus-package dollars the U.S. government is investing in green energy development.

The two proposals emphasize different primary goals. The first sees our dependence on other nations for something essential to our functioning and well-being as a national security issue. Global warming is acknowledged as a problem, but is of less immediate concern than our dependence on foreign oil. The second proposal sees global warming as an immediate crisis that needs to be addressed now for the ecological well-being of all of us, including the global community. Our dependence on foreign oil diminishes as we aggressively implement green energy alternatives.

By now you can likely guess which proposal I lean into. Supporting a plan that benefits me and my fellow citizens but contributes harm to others who share earth with me does not fit with my commitment to walk gently. Besides, it's not like there are *our* problems and *their* problems—*all* problems belong to *all* of us. We are (humans and nonhumans alike) connected and interdependent. For any one nation's security to depend on a plan that the global scientific community says undermines the well-being of people in Africa and Southeast Asia today, and will undermine the well-being of our grandchildren tomorrow, is short-sighted, and denies our fundamental unity. Our best national security will be built on sustainable energy solutions that consider the well-being of all life, and foster collaborative and strong international relationships. I wouldn't stand where I stand with confidence or hope if I hadn't seen viable alternatives and hopeful stories.

# ACKNOWLEDGMENTS

Many people have infused our lives with wisdom, kindness and guidance, bringing us to greater understanding and compassion on issues of creation care. We thank the following people whose influence has shaped not only the pages of this book but also the directions of our lives.

## MEGAN ANNA

The World Relief Malawi staff inspired me through their tireless work alongside the church to bring the kingdom of God to their neighbors through agriculture, HIV/AIDS education, and health and child development initiatives.

Inspiration and my belief in the power of the gospel comes from my experience with The African Church, an independent church in northern Malawi. I witnessed the poor caring for the orphans and widows in their community, and a community where the gospel was profoundly at work forming and shaping people. This community gives me hope that the gospel can shape our communities and churches and help us walk gently.

Paul Robinson, director of the HNGR department at Wheaton College, was integral in installing an awareness of and passion for global Christianity and deepening my understanding of the responsibility and beauty of working toward the kingdom of God.

The Church of Christ in Ghana welcomed me and taught me

about West African Christianity. Particular thanks goes to my teachers there: Reverend George Kwapong and Reverend Solomon Anokye Nkansah, and to Professor Kofi Asare Opoku, who introduced me to Akan proverbs and the richness of African traditional religions.

I thank Dr. Cephas Omenyo, my professor at Princeton Theological Seminary who inspired me to deepen my appreciation of the wisdom inherent in Christianity.

And finally, I am thankful for the support and encouragement of my husband, Luke, who is my best friend and best editor.

## LISA

Quakers have long valued God's creation and seen our role as that of partner-steward, charged to protect and bring to fruition the fullness of God's creation. My father also taught me to cherish and enjoy God's creation, and gave me permission to love it all, and in his memory, I thank him for the hikes, star-gazing nights and tender care of broken birds.

Two students and two friends read and responded to portions of the manuscript, helping make it a better book: Hannah Flegal, Pamela Lau, Kari Wagner and Mauri Macy. Authors who have been instrumental in developing my thoughts on these matters deserve noting as well, particularly Bill McKibben, Lester Brown, Barbara Kingsolver, Janisse Ray, Wendell Berry and Leopold Aldo.

We also thank IVP, our publisher, who took the risk for this book, and provided support, encouragement and guidance along the way, especially through our editor, Cindy Bunch, and associate publisher Jeff Crosby. The book is better because of their commitment to it.

As always, I can't imagine writing a book without the encouragement, feedback and love of my lifelong partner, cofarmer, cowalker, co-just-about-everything, Mark.

# NOTES

**Prelude: Siamese Crocodiles**

*page 10*    "We cannot bear": Charles W. Forman, *A Faith for the Nations* (Philadelphia: Westminster Press, 1957), pp. 19-20.

*page 11*    Forman recounts the story of Augustine: Ibid., p. 29.

**Chapter 1: For the Beauty of the Earth**

*page 15*    The debate about whether or not global warming: Eli Kintisch and Richard A. Kerr, "Global Warming, Hotter Than Ever," *Science* 318, no. 5858 (2007): 1846-47.

*page 16*    2.7 million trees were to be planted: The Nature Conservatory is working with local partners to replant 2.5 million acres of the Brazilian Atlantic Forest, reconnecting more than 12 million acres of the forest. See <www.bizjournals.com/losangeles/stories/2009/04/27/daily24.html>, accessed in May 2009.

*page 17*    an average of forty miles a day: Based on U.S. government statistics, cars are driven an average of fifteen thousand miles per year.

*page 18*    African professor and theologian J. O. Y. Mante says: J. O. Y Mante, *Africa: Theological and Philosophical Roots of Our Ecological Crises* (Accra, Ghana: SonLife Press, 2004).

*page 20*    Noticing and loving creation reflects respect: Steven Bouma-Prediger unpacks this in his book *For the Beauty of the Earth: A Christian Vision for Creation Care* (Grand Rapids: Baker Academic, 2001), p. 141.

*page 20*    "God's creatures are valuable not because": Ibid., p. 142.

*page 24*    "Instead of exercising our dominion": Nate Jones, "Gardening in the Cracks," *Books & Culture* (March/April 2009): 21.

*page 25*    Arthur Roberts pictures a new earth: Arthur Roberts, *Explor-*

*ing Heaven: What Great Christian Thinkers Tell Us About Our Afterlife with God* (San Francisco: HarperCollins, 2003)..

*page 26*   sifting through reliable sources: Determining the credibility of Internet sources can be challenging. I tend to consider the information on U.S. government sites (.gov) accurate, and educational sites (.edu) credible. One way to determine the credibility of .org sites is to Google the organization and read what you can about it. This would also be true of .com sites, though I use them least of all, as I imagine mostly they are trying to sell me something.

## Prelude: Strength Lies in Unity

*page 31*   Due to our reason and ability: J. O. Y Mante, *Africa: Theological and Philosophical Roots of Our Ecological Crises* (Accra, Ghana: SonLife Press, 2004), p. 52.

*page 31*   a male chick hatched: Erik Marcus, *Vegan: The New Ethics of Eating* (Ithaca, N.Y.: McBooks, 2001), pp. 112-14.

*page 31*   Since the well-being of people: John Taylor, *The Primal Vision* (London: SCM Press, 1963), pp. 66-67.

## Chapter 2: Farming Practices

*page 33*   According to the U.S. Department of Agriculture: See <www .ers.usda.gov/publications/eib3/charts.htm>.

*page 37*   We could have driven to U-Pick farms: See <www.pick yourown.org> to find farms near you offering u-pick.

*page 42*   This nurturing animal is the most mistreated: Michael Pollan's book *The Omnivore's Dilemma* (New York: Penguin Books, 2006) is only one place where this particular issue is unpacked; the Humane Society provides more extensive information and action possibilities. See the resources at the end of the chapter.

*page 42*   Between half and two-thirds of her beak: The practice is held by some poultry scientists and factory representatives to not be painful, but a group of veterinarians who explored debeaking extensively as part of a task force set for Parliament concluded that debeaking was painful and cruel. See the United Poultry Concerns for more information: <www .upc-online.org/merchandise/debeak_factsheet.html> (accessed August 2009).

*page 43*   that single pound of beef: See John Robbins, "2,500 Gallons All

Wet?" at <www.earthsave.org/environment/water.htm> (re-
trieved February 2009). This number has been debated. The
cattlemen say it takes about 840 gallons per pound, which includes irrigating land for grain and hay to feed the cows. The
Water Education Foundation says 2,464. Other estimates are as
high as 6,000 gallons per pound. Even if it did take only 840
gallons per pound, that's still an amazing amount of water for a
pound of beef. According to Robbins, nearly half of the water
consumed in our country is used for livestock—primarily beef.

*page 44*       foodlike products: All of Michael Pollan's books about food
and the food industry are excellent for anyone looking for
good discussions on food.

*page 44*       Monoculture agribusiness made an extra five hundred calories: See Michael Pollan's discussion of this in *The Omnivore's
Dilemma.*

*page 48*       neighbors are coming together to plant: The American Community Gardening Association, started in 1979, is an organization aimed at building community health through community gardens in the United States and Canada. According to
Amy DeShon, executive director of the American Community
Gardening Association (ACGA), eighteen thousand to twenty
thousand community gardens bloom in cities throughout the
United States, which is a 35 percent increase over five years
ago (from an interview with Amy DeShon, April 2008).

*page 50*       John Peck, executive director of Family Farm Defenders: John
Peck, "Why Food Sovereignty Matters," *World Ark* (October
2007): 28-29.

*page 51*       Since the establishment of the North American Free Trade
Agreement: Ibid.

*page 53*       I'm comfortably situated in the upper-middle class: Though
I'd like to claim middle middle class—as would most Americans—I squirm when I realize my income puts me enough
above the median U.S. family income of $52,000 that I can't
pretend to be middle middle class.

*page 55*       Mike and Jill are committed: See <www.gaininggroundfarm
.com/family.html> where they describe their feed-a-family
program.

*pages 55-56*   "The majority of Americans buy bottled drinking water": Barbara Kingsolver, *Animal, Vegetable, Miracle: A Year of Food Life*
(San Francisco: HarperCollins, 2007), pp. 115-16.

Chapter 3: Dining at Tables of Compassion

*page 69*        The Hebrew noun *shalom* describes a peace: Terry McGonigal,
                 dean of spiritual life at Whitworth University, unpacked the
                 biblical uses of the term *shalom* at the George Fox University
                 faculty retreat, "If You Only Knew What Would Bring Peace:
                 Shalom Theology as the Biblical Foundation for Diversity,"
                 August 2009.

*page 70*        We will not turn away from the suffering: See <www.global
                 exchange.org/campaigns/fairtrade/cocoa/background.html>
                 for a good history of the cocoa industry in Africa (accessed
                 July 2009).

*page 70*        Seeking justice means we will learn something: Micah Chal-
                 lenge USA is a great beginning point for learning about what's
                 being done and what can be done to address global issues of
                 justice. See <www.micahchallenge.us>.

*page 71*        better access to water, seeds and tools: David Lane, "The Cam-
                 paign to Make Poverty History," letter sent from ONE, April
                 16, 2007.

*page 71*        the top priority they voiced: Conversation with Jason Fileta,
                 coordinator of Micah Challenge USA, held September 2009.

*page 72*        Multinational corporations (MNCs) like Dole, Nestlé, Folgers
                 and Del Monte: For an example of the abuses in the cocoa
                 industry, see <www.corpwatch.org/article.php?id=12754>
                 (accessed July 2009).

*page 72*        Most coffee farmers in Kenya: Joyce Mulama, "Development-
                 Kenya: Coffee Profits Not Percolating Down to Farmers,"
                 2006 <www.ipsnews.net/africa/nota.asp?idnews=33153> (ac-
                 cessed March 2008).

*page 74*        evidence that trade can be a path: Fair Trade Federation,
                 J. Cavanagh, "Why Fair Trade? A Brief Look at Fair-Trade in
                 the Global Economy" <www.fairtradefederation.org/ab_
                 whyft.html> (accessed October 2007).

*page 74*        The goal is to free people economically: Fair Trade Certified—
                 Frequently Asked Questions <www.transfairusa.org/content/
                 resources/faq.php> (accessed October 2007).

*page 75*        "tragic political and social consequences": "At Rome summit,
                 Ban urges 'bold and urgent' steps to tackle global food crisis,"
                 UN News Centre <www.un.org/apps/news/story.asp?NewsID
                 =26890&Cr=food&Cr1=crisis> (accessed June 2008).

*page 76*        California is the fifth largest: Iowa is the number-one egg-producing state, followed by Ohio, Indiana, Pennsylvania and then California. The top five states produce half of all eggs produced in the United States. See <www.unitedegg.org/us eggindustry_generalstats.aspx> for a complete rundown (accessed July 2009).

*page 77*     Whole Foods and Trader Joe's deal: Visit The Human Society website to find out about more companies switching to cage-free eggs: <www.hsus.org/farm/resources/animals/chickens/> (accessed June 2008).

*page 81*     In the United States we make our way through 17,600 pounds: Biing-Hwan Lin and Steven T. Yen, "The U.S. Grain Consumption Landscape: Who Eats Grain, in What Form, Where, and How Much?" summary of an Economic Research Service report of the U.S. Department of Agriculture, November 2007 <www.ers.usda.gov/publications/err50/err50_reportsummary.pdf> (accessed March 2009).

*page 81*     if everyone ate the diet of an average U.S. citizen: Lester Brown, *Plan B 3.0: Mobilizing to Save Civilization* (New York: Norton, 2008), p. 188. The calculation used here is based on the amount of grain used per person annually for food and feed.

*page 86*     one of the most human-rights-abusing industries: See the International Labor Rights Forum for background and current information about child labor and slavery in the chocolate industry: <www.laborrights.org/stop-child-labor/cocoa-campaign> (accessed May 2009).

## Chapter 4: Living in the Marketplace

*page 100*    A number of groups rank corporations: Corporate Responsibility Officer (CRO) releases the 100 Best Corporate Citizens every year, and *Fortune* magazine lists the best and the worst companies (the Fortune 500). The Motley Fool comes up with its own list as well. Each of them focuses on different values, and so what determines good citizenry is a bit subjective, but lists such as these at least let companies know they are being watched.

*page 101*    In 2004 Starbucks joined the UN Global Compact: For the Starbucks plan and report, go to <www.starbucks.com/sharedplanet/index.aspx> (accessed August 2009).

*page 109*    Financial guru Dave Ramsey: Dave Ramsey supports a webpage that makes his basic principles available to the public. He also has written books. See <www.DaveRamsey.com> (accessed August 2009).

page 110    the broadly criticized Walmart corporation: See <www.green americatoday.org> for more information on this and other corporations, or see the documentary, *Walmart: The High Cost of Low Price* (2005), which explores the dark side of Walmart. The Web address <www.walmartmovie.com> takes you to the hosting site and includes updates.

page 112    Yes, we can get our clothes, dishes: For recipes go to <www .eartheasy.com/live_nontoxic_solutions.htm> (accessed August 2009).

page 112    There is also the Lethal Dose (LD) test: See the In Defense of Animals website for more information about this and other animal abuse issues: <www.idausa.org/facts/costesting.html> (accessed August 2009).

page 112    Otherwise the European Union may not have voted: The vote took place in 2009; the full effect of the ban will be in place by 2013.

page 113    We can purchase carpets manufactured: Ray Anderson is the CEO of Interface. Once he saw how much pollution his business contributed to, he turned the company around in fifteen years, decreasing carbon emissions and the amount of water used to make carpets, and instigating a recycling program for old carpets (from either Interface or other manufacturers) to keep them out of landfills. Anderson has encouraged other CEOs to do the same and has been a model of what's possible. You can look the company up at <www.interfaceglobal.com/ Sustainability.aspx> or, for an outsider's opinion, go to <www .centerforsustainability.org/resources.php?category=224& root=176>.

### Prelude: God Is in the Heavens

page 123    The Hebrew worldview in the Old Testament: George Kehm, "The New Story," in *After Nature's Revolt*, ed. Dieter Hessel (Minneapolis: Fortress, 1992), pp. 97-98.

page 123    When our theology focuses more on God's plan: Syd Hielema, "Searching for 'Disconnected Wires': Karl Barth's Doctrine of Creation Revisited," *Calvin Theological Journal* 30, no. 1 (1995): 77.

## Chapter 5: A Matter of Degrees

page 127    Richard Kerr, an oceanographer and senior writer: Richard A. Kerr, "Climate Change: Global Warming Is Changing the World," *Sciénce* 316, no. 5822 (2007): 188-90.

page 127    In February of 2009 Field addressed the American Science: "Global Warming 'Underestimated,'" BBC NEWS, Science & Environment <http://news.bbc.co.uk/2/hi/science/nature/78 90988.stm> (accessed February 2009).

page 128    Movements like 350.org: 350 parts of $CO_2$ per million is the concentration determined by climatologists that allows the world to function as it has—to be the same kind of world tomorrow that we were born into yesterday. We are at 390 ppm, so we have some backpeddling to do, and the scientific community says we have to do it fast.

page 128    Ordinary people planned: See <www.350.org> to learn about the ongoing efforts to mobilize the planet, as well as a history of the group.

page 128    Others, like Harrison Schmitt, an Apollo 17 astronaut: "Ex-Astronaut: Global Warming Is Bunk," FoxNews.com, Associated Press, February 16, 2009 <www.foxnews.com/story/0,2933,493624,00.html> (accessed February 2009).

page 128    2008 was the coolest year: Although 2008 was the coolest year since 2000, according to climatologists at the NASA Goddard Institute for Space Studies, 2008 was the nineth warmest year since 1980.

page 130    Oriana Zill de Granados found: Oriana Zill de Granados, "The Doubters of Global Warming," Frontline, April 2007 <www.pbs.org/wgbh/pages/frontline/hotpolitics/reports/skeptics.html> (accessed July 2008).

page 130    the larger group of climatologists, meteorologists: Real climate.org is a blog maintained by scientists who are debunking the claims made by global warming skeptics as they show up in various academic articles and popular magazines and on talk shows.

page 132    A lot of folks are assuming so: 350.org is a global movement that sent a clear message to world leaders on October 24, 2009—a global day of action—communicating that the peoples of the world wanted to see significant policy come out of the global climate change talks at the UN Climate Change Conference in Copenhagen in December of 2009.

*page 133*  In 1850 scientists began using thermometers: Global warming conversations begin by looking at the warming and cooling trends at least since 1850, which turn out to be a lot more about warming than cooling. Other climate study reports using the geological record suggest that the twenty years from 1980 to 2000 were the hottest in the last four hundred years and possibly the warmest for several thousand. Both of these types of data (thermometer readings that anyone can evaluate, and geological studies most of us can't) tell us that the earth is warming, and the rate of warming is increasing.

*page 133*  Earth has moved from glacial periods: Scientists who look at orbiting patterns of earth say we might have another fifty thousand years to enjoy this moderate climate before the next ice age, though interglacial periods typically last about twelve thousand years, a fact that may be more troubling to our great-great-grandchildren than it is to most of us.

*page 134*  those who believe the earth is less than ten thousand: I wonder if some of our difficulty believing in an earth that is millions of years older than humanity is that we have a hard time imagining the *point* of earth existing so long without humans! Especially if we were supposed to be in charge of it all. It's a humbling thought. Indeed, if humans haven't been around as long as, say, the Atlantic Ocean, then maybe we ought to feel a bit more humble about the way we have expanded into creation, and recognize there is a significant backstory to this place—a place God loved, sustained and delighted in long before humans entered the picture. Maybe God knew that the unique capacities humans would have meant our time on earth needed to be limited, so that all of creation might flourish for a good while before we came into our strength in ways that compromised earth's life-flourishing capacities. Just a thought . . .

*page 135*  Greenhouse gases come from: We also release methane from growing rice, stirring up swampy lands, coal mining and burning natural gas, and from gathering high quantities of animal feces in one place, such as occurs at Concentrated Animal Feeding Operations (CAFOs). Nitrous oxide is released mostly from our fertilizers and agricultural practices.

*page 136*  The fact is, earth once had a heck of a lot more trees: At the beginning of the twentieth century five billion hectares of forest covered the earth; now it's just under four billion. We gain and lose some each year—with plantings on the gain side, and continued deforestation on the loss side. The net forest loss worldwide is more than seven million hectares per year. For a more detailed accounting see Lester Brown, *Plan B 3.0: Mobilizing to Save Civilization* (New York: W.W. Norton, 2008). This book is available as a free download at <www.earth-policy.org/Books/PB3/>.

*page 136*    A 2007 United Nations study concluded: Austin Gelder and Lauren Wilcox, "The Carbon Hoofprint," *World Ark* (May/June 2008): 18-26.

*page 138*    Ice caps covered the north: The Ward Hunt Ice Shelf is a specific example of the meltdown. For three thousand years this block of ice (the largest in the Arctic) did its work of reflecting the sun and fostering a rather unique ecosystem up north. In 2002 graduate student Derek Mueller found evidence that the shelf had split all the way through, suddenly draining a large freshwater lake into the ocean. Now the Ward Hunt Ice Shelf is breaking into pieces, raising the level of oceans and no longer functioning as a viable habitat for local animals or as a cooling agent for earth. See <http://earthobservatory.nasa.gov/study/wardhunt> for the full story (accessed March 2010).

*page 138*    climate change effects are already being significantly felt: See <www.nrdc.org/globalWarming/qthinice.asp> for more information (accessed July 2008).

*page 139*    Due to its geographic location, Bangladesh has already experienced: Climate Change and Bangladesh, September 2007, report produced for the UN Environment Programme on Climate Change by Dr. Fakhruddin Ahmed of the People's Republic of Bangladesh. For a full report see <www.un.org/webcast/climatechange/.../2007/pdfs/bangladesh-eng.pdf> (accessed March 2010).

*page 139*    We live in constant fear of the adverse impacts: See <www.tuvaluislands.com/warming.htm> (accessed March 2009).

*page 140*    we ought to step back and reconsider: Nations and leaders of the world are listening to the international community of researchers who agree on climate change. The IPCC has been at work for over fifteen years assessing and developing policy recommendations. The panel includes summaries for policy-makers that were agreed on by governmental delegates from about one hundred countries—including all the world's major countries. No other scientific topic has been so thoroughly researched and reviewed. Those who have studied this topic most extensively say that if we don't choose a different path now, we will be forced to choose between fewer choices later.

*page 141*  People and organizations around the world expressed: The roots for 350.org started with teacher and environmentalist Bill McKibben and six college seniors at Middlebury College who won the support of their elected representatives by walking across Vermont to voice their concern that government officials get serious about climate change. By the time they arrived at the capitol one thousand people stood with them. Inspired by their success they established 350.org, which takes this action global.

*page 143*  Climatologists watching the ozone layer depletion: See <www .theozonehole.com/montreal.htm> (accessed July 2008).

*page 143*  the Kyoto Protocol: The Kyoto Protocol is an international agreement to reduce carbon emissions adopted in 1997 and entered into force in 2005. One hundred and eighty-five countries have signed the Kyoto Protocol, agreeing to move beyond encouraging change to making commitments that involve being held accountable for reaching set goals.

*page 144*  China offers one example of the unsustainability: Brown, *Plan B 3.0*, pp. 13-14.

*page 146*  If each of us in the United States replaced: For more info see <www.energystar.gov/ia/partners/promotions/change_light/ downloads/Fact_Sheet_Mercury.pdf> (accessed May 2009).

*page 146*  That one change does the world: The incentives are helping overcome some of the initial resistance to the bulbs. Part of the concern was about the mercury in CFL bulbs. The newest reduced-mercury bulbs have about 1.4 to 2.5 milligrams in them; the older CFL bulbs contained about 4 milligrams of mercury. By way of comparison, the glass thermometers I used to check my daughters' fevers had about 500 milligrams of mercury in them. Still, no loose mercury is good mercury, and the bulbs should be handled carefully and recycled so that the mercury can be recaptured, rather than released to the atmosphere. Another part of the resistance has been the price of the CFL bulbs and LEDs. Even if we can be convinced that we will save money in the long run on both the price of bulbs and our electricity bill, it's *today* we think about as we swipe our card or hand over our money. To address this, Prescott proposed removing the price advantage of incandescent bulbs by substantially decreasing the sales tax on CFL bulbs and LEDs in Great Britain, and by increasing the price for incandescent bulbs to make it more reflective of the real cost to society of using them. He also proposed helping low-income citizens replace their incandescent bulbs, perhaps with the funds raised by increasing the cost of incandescent bulbs, and encouraging the responsible recycling of all those now-undesirable bulbs.

*page 147*     If we all recycled paper as effectively as South Korea: Brown, *Plan B 3.0*, p. 53. We recycle about 50 percent of our paper in the United States—which isn't bad.

*pages 147-48*  The European Union has good reason to feel optimistic: Reforesting areas for carbon sequestering is one important part of the Kyoto Protocol. See <http://unfccc.int/kyoto_protocol/items/2830.php> for more information.

*page 148*     A University of Helsinki study found: "European Union Forests Expanding, Absorbing Carbon at Surprisingly High Rate," *Science Daily*, November 29, 2007 <www.sciencedaily.com/releases/2007/11/071129113752.htm> (accessed August 2008).

*page 148*     Reducing the net loss of trees around the world: See <www.worldwildlife.org/what/globalmarkets/forests/index.html> (accessed August 2008).

### Prelude: The Earth Has Weight
*pages 154-55*  "when orphanages were needed in North America": Sarah McFarland Taylor, *Green Sisters* (Cambridge, Mass.: Harvard University Press, 2000), p. 2.

*page 155*     The Green Sisters are the new "missionaries": Ibid., p. ix.
*page 155*     They use their communal lands: Ibid., p. 196.
*page 155*     As Sister Elizabeth Walters from Hope Takes Root: Ibid., p. 192.

### Chapter 6: Fuels That Fire Our Engines
*page 157*     According to the Earth Hour Media Centre: "Earth Hour's Countdown to Copenhagen," April 3, 2009 <www.earthhour

.org/Media.aspx> (accessed May 2009).

*page 161*    A home audit helped in figuring out: For home audit resources go to <www.energysavers.gov/your_home/energy_audits/index.cif/mytopic=11170>.

*page 161*    You can hire an energy rater: Check the Yellow Pages for energy raters, or go to <www.natresnet.org> for a directory of accredited companies nationwide.

*page 161*    The average person in the United States emits: See <http://maps.grida.no/go/graphic/co2-emissions-per-person-in-latin-america-and-the-caribbean-compared-to-the-world-and-oecd-average-emissions> for a helpful comparison table of a number of countries (accessed March 2009).

*page 162*    If you have a boiler and need to replace it: This is considerably easier if you live in the United Kingdom, though I'm hopeful the trend will cross the Atlantic soon. Biomass boilers for businesses, hospitals and schools are available in the United States now, and wood- and biomass-burning furnaces and stoves are available for residential use.

*page 163*    Portland General Electric (PGE) residential renewable power program: PGE Renewable Power Program, 121 SW Salmon St., Portland, OR 97204. Access updated information from <www.GreenPowerOregon.com>.

*page 166*    Germany has cut its coal use by 37 percent: Lester Brown, *Plan B 3.0: Mobilizing to Save Civilization* (New York: W. W. Norton, 2008), p. 215.

*page 166*    In 2007 the Oregon legislature passed: See <http://oregon.gov/ENERGY/RENEW/docs/FinalREAP.pdf> (accessed September 2008).

## Chapter 7: Sustaining the Blessing of Families

*page 183*    Like Dr. Seuss's Mayzie the lazy bird: See Dr. Seuss's classic children's book *Horton Hatches the Egg*, first published in 1940.

*page 183*    Estimates put the world population between 150 and 300 million: See, for example, John H. Tanton, "End of the Migration Epoch," reprinted by *The Social Contract Press* 5, no. 1 (1994).

*page 185*    Mormons still tend to have larger families: Rodney Stark and Roger Finke, *Acts of Faith: Explaining the Human Side of Religion* (Berkeley: University of California Press, 2000), pp. 49-50.

*page 190*    What if I could watch the suffering in Honduras: See Dan

Koeppel's book *Banana: The Fate of the Fruit That Changed the World* (New York: Hudson Street Press, 2007) for a good history of the banana industry.

page 192     In 1969 President Nixon established a population commission: The 1972 Rockefeller Commission Report on U.S. Population <www.dieoff.org/page73.htm> (accessed January 2009).

page 193     QuiverFull is a movement: See <www.quiverfull.com> for the group's website.

page 194     In *The Theology of the Body*, Pope John Paul II reaffirmed: See Pope John Paul II's *Theology of the Body* (Boston: Pauline Books & Media, 1997) for a recapping of the Church's position, and a reaffirmation of it.

### Prelude: It Is God Who Swats the Flies for the Tailless Pig

page 202     I grew up with the idea that the imago Dei: Andrew Louth, ed., *Genesis 1–11*, Ancient Christian Commentary on Scripture (Downers Grove, Ill.: InterVarsity Press, 2002), p. 27.

page 202     Subduing creation was for the sole sake: James Murphy, *Commentary on the Book of Genesis* (Boston: Estes and Lauriat, 1873), p. 65.

page 203     we *represent* God on earth through our actions: For more information see Willem VanGemeren, ed., *New International Dictionary of Old Testament Theology and Exegesis*, vol. 1 (Grand Rapids: Zondervan, 1997), pp. 969-70.

page 203     Human dominion is to be a benevolent: Bernhard Anderson, *Contours of Old Testament Theology* (Minneapolis: Fortress, 1998), p. 91.

page 205     "Wherever the African is": John Mbiti, *African Religions and Philosophy* (Portsmouth, N.H.: Heinemann, 1969), p. 2.

page 206     When Israel is in bondage to Egypt: Sylvia Keesmaat, "Exodus and the Intertextual Transformation of Tradition in Romans 8.14-30," *Journal for the Study of the New Testament* 16, no. 54 (1994): 43-44.

page 206     The prophet Jeremiah speaks most clearly: Terence Fretheim, "The Earth Story in Jeremiah 12," in *Readings from the Perspective of Earth*, ed. Norman Habel (Cleveland: Sheffield Academic, 2000), p. 100.

### Appendix B: A Primer on Traditional Energy Sources

page 218     According to the Illinois Office of Coal Development and

Marketing: See <www.commerce.state.il.us/dceo/Bureaus/ Coal/> (accessed October 2008).

*page 218*  comparison of the United States and France in sources of electricity: Charts breaking down sources of electricity in the U.S. and France are available on Wikipedia. Data from the Department of Energy were used in their construction. See <http://en.wikipedia.org/wiki/electricity_generation> (accessed March 2010).

*page 219*  Natural gas burns cleaner: See the EIA for the most recent and thorough data on energy use: <http://eia.doe.gov/international /RecentNaturalGasOverview.xls> (accessed September 2008).

*page 219*  The United States has a fairly good supply: According to the EIA we exported fifty-nine million tons in 2007, and imported thirty-six million tons (U.S. Coal Supply & Demand, April 2008 Report <www.eia.doe.gov/cneaf/coal/page/special/feature .html>, accessed September 2008).

*page 219*  One of the agreement points: EIA, Official Energy Statistics from the U.S. Government, updated February 2009, <www .eia.doe.gov/basics/quickoil.html> (accessed May 2009). It is also worth noting that in 2006 (the most recent year for which EIA data is available) the total world oil production was 82.5 million barrels/day, while the total world petroleum consumption was nearly 85 million barrels/day.